SQL Mastery: From Novice Queries to Advanced Database Wizardry

Table of Contents

Chapter 1: Introduction to SQL and Databases

- Understanding what SQL is and its importance in database management.

- Overview of database types and how SQL fits into the ecosystem.

Chapter 2: Setting Up Your SQL Environment

- Installing SQL Server, MySQL, or PostgreSQL on your machine.

- Setting up a database and connecting to it using SQL clients.

Chapter 3: First Steps: The Basic SQL Syntax

- Writing your first SELECT statements to retrieve data.

- Understanding SQL keywords, clauses, and operators.

Chapter 4: Filtering Data: WHERE Clauses and Operators

- Using the WHERE clause to filter query results.

- Exploring comparison and logical operators for more precise queries.

Chapter 5: Sorting Data: ORDER BY and LIMIT

- Sorting results using ORDER BY for ascending and descending order.

- Using LIMIT (or TOP) to restrict query results to a specific number.

Chapter 6: Aggregating Data: COUNT, SUM, AVG, MIN, and MAX

- How to use aggregation functions to summarize data.

- Grouping data for more meaningful analysis with GROUP BY.

Chapter 7: Joins: Combining Data from Multiple Tables

- Introduction to INNER JOIN, LEFT JOIN, RIGHT JOIN, and FULL JOIN.

- Understanding how joins work and optimizing queries with multiple tables.

Chapter 8: Subqueries and Nested Queries

- Writing subqueries within SELECT, WHERE, and FROM clauses.

- Optimizing queries with nested SELECT statements for complex data retrieval.

Chapter 9: Data Modification: INSERT, UPDATE, and DELETE

- Learning to insert, modify, and delete records in your database.

- Using transactions to ensure data integrity during updates.

Chapter 10: Working with Constraints and Indexes

- Understanding primary keys, foreign keys, and unique constraints.

- The role of indexes in optimizing query performance.

Chapter 11: Data Normalization and Database Design

- The importance of normalizing data to reduce redundancy.

- Best practices for designing efficient and scalable databases.

Chapter 12: Advanced Query Techniques: CASE Statements and CTEs

- Using CASE statements for conditional logic within queries.

- Exploring Common Table Expressions (CTEs) for better query organization.

Chapter 13: Functions and Stored Procedures

- Writing and using built-in SQL functions for custom calculations.

- Understanding stored procedures to encapsulate SQL logic.

Chapter 14: Triggers and Events

- Defining triggers to automate actions in response to database events.

- Creating scheduled events for automated database maintenance tasks.

Chapter 15: Working with Views

- What are views, and how do they simplify complex queries?

- Creating, updating, and deleting views in your SQL database.

Chapter 16: Data Security and Permissions

- Securing your database with user roles and permissions.

- Best practices for maintaining data integrity and preventing unauthorized access.

Chapter 17: Transactions and Isolation Levels

- Understanding transactions and the ACID properties.

- Working with different isolation levels to control concurrent transactions.

Chapter 18: Advanced Join Techniques: Self-Joins and Cross Joins

- Exploring self-joins to query hierarchical data.

- Using cross joins for generating combinations of result sets.

Chapter 19: Query Optimization and Execution Plans

- How SQL optimizes queries and understanding execution plans.

- Tips and tricks for improving query performance through indexing and query structure.

Chapter 20: Working with Large Datasets

- Techniques for handling and querying massive amounts of data.

- Using partitioning and window functions for improved efficiency.

Chapter 21: Full-Text Search and Advanced Filtering

- Using full-text search for complex pattern matching.

- Exploring advanced filtering techniques with regular expressions.

Chapter 22: Data Backup, Recovery, and High Availability

- The importance of data backup strategies and disaster recovery.

- Setting up high availability options for SQL databases.

Chapter 23: SQL Server Management Tools and GUI Interfaces

- Using SQL Server Management Studio (SSMS) and other database tools.

- Exploring graphical interfaces for easier query building and administration.

Chapter 24: SQL for Data Warehousing and Business Intelligence

- Using SQL for ETL processes and managing data warehouses.

- Advanced SQL for integrating with business intelligence (BI) tools.

Chapter 25: Best Practices, Debugging, and Future SQL Trends

- SQL coding best practices for readability, performance, and security.

- Looking forward to new SQL features and the evolving landscape of database management.

Chapter 1: Introduction to SQL and Databases

Ah, databases! The unsung heroes of the digital world. We interact with them daily, whether we're scrolling through Instagram, checking our bank balance, or browsing our favorite online stores. Yet, most of us are blissfully unaware of the complex systems running behind the scenes to make all that magic happen. This chapter is here to pull back the curtain, and show you the powerful yet humble language that brings it all together: SQL (Structured Query Language). If you've ever wondered how websites manage millions of users, how apps store their data, or how companies analyze customer behavior, SQL is likely the key. In this chapter, we'll go over the basics of SQL and databases, starting with the essential concepts that even the most seasoned programmers need to understand. Buckle up, because we're about to embark on a journey into the world of data storage, retrieval, and manipulation. It's less like "Matrix"-style hacking and more like a digital wizardry that takes place on your computer's hard drive. Ready? Let's dive in.

So, what exactly is a database? Imagine a filing cabinet. But instead of paper files, it's all digital, and each "file" is structured data—rows and columns. You might recognize this format as a table. Yes, the database is essentially a super-organized filing system where data is neatly arranged and easily accessible. Whether it's storing your movie recommendations, cataloging your favorite books, or keeping track of an online store's inventory, databases help keep everything in order. But unlike a filing cabinet where papers can get lost or scattered, databases are designed to store, retrieve, and manage massive amounts of data efficiently. And the best part? You can easily update, search, and manipulate that data without worrying about losing a single scrap of information—no dust, no disorganization, just clean, structured data that's easy to find. SQL is the key to interacting with that data. It's like the magic spell you use to get the filing cabinet to open, find exactly what you need, and then perform operations on that data without any hassle.

SQL, or Structured Query Language, is a programming language specifically designed to interact with relational databases. A relational database organizes data into tables, each of which can be linked to other tables through relationships. Think of it as a set of connected spreadsheets—each table containing related information, but working together in harmony. For example, in an online store, there might be one table for customers, one for products, and one for orders. The order table could be linked to both the customer and product tables by using something called a "primary key" and a "foreign key." The primary key uniquely identifies each record in a table, while the foreign key links one table to another. SQL allows you to run queries (commands) on these tables to retrieve, update, insert, or delete data. Need a list of all the orders made by a particular customer? SQL's got your back. It's as if you could shout at your filing cabinet, "Give me all the orders from Steve, please!" and voilà, there they are.

Now that we have an idea of what SQL is and how databases work, let's talk about what makes SQL so special. First, SQL is highly readable. It uses plain English keywords that even someone with little to no programming experience can understand. For example, the SQL command `SELECT * FROM customers` is almost self-explanatory: "Select everything (the asterisk) from the customers table." The command `UPDATE orders SET status = 'shipped' WHERE order_id = 123` is just as intuitive: "Update the orders table, set the status to 'shipped' where the order ID is 123." Sure, there's some technical syntax, but for the most part, SQL reads like an easily understandable language. It's not like trying to decipher ancient runes—SQL is a straightforward and user-friendly tool for accessing and modifying data in databases.

But of course, don't let its user-friendly syntax fool you. SQL is powerful. It can handle complex queries with ease, retrieving and processing data from multiple tables, aggregating information, and even performing calculations on that data. This is where SQL truly shines. You can use it to gather insights from massive datasets that would be otherwise difficult to analyze. For instance, let's say you run an online clothing store. You can use SQL to query sales data, group orders by customer demographics, and calculate average order values by region. Or perhaps you want to analyze product sales trends over time, broken down by category. No problem! SQL allows you to perform this analysis with just a few lines of code. And the best part? You don't need to be a data scientist to get meaningful results—SQL makes complex operations accessible to everyone.

Speaking of complex queries, let's talk about "joins." A join is a type of SQL operation that allows you to combine data from two or more tables based on a related column. Imagine this: You have one table for customers and another table for orders. Each order in the orders table is associated with a specific customer in the customers table. With a simple SQL join, you can pull all the orders for a particular customer in one neat query. There are several types of joins— INNER JOIN, LEFT JOIN, RIGHT JOIN, and FULL JOIN—and each has its own use case. For example, an INNER JOIN retrieves data that exists in both tables, while a LEFT JOIN will return all records from the left table, along with matching records from the right table. Joins can sound a bit confusing at first, but once you get the hang of them, you'll be pulling data from multiple tables like a pro. They're one of the most powerful tools in SQL's arsenal.

Another key feature of SQL is its ability to filter data. Sometimes, you don't want to retrieve all the data from a table—maybe you're only interested in a subset of records. SQL's `WHERE` clause lets you filter records based on certain conditions. For example, if you want to retrieve a list of orders that were placed in the last 30 days, you can write a query like this: `SELECT * FROM orders WHERE order_date > NOW() - INTERVAL 30 DAY`. The `WHERE` clause filters the data, returning only records that meet your criteria. You can even combine multiple conditions using logical operators like `AND` and `OR`. This filtering ability is crucial for working with large datasets, where you don't always want to retrieve every single row.

SQL doesn't just let you query and retrieve data—it also lets you modify and manage it. With SQL, you can insert new records into a table, update existing ones, and delete rows that are no longer needed. If you've ever used a web application where you had to update your contact information or change your password, you can bet that SQL was involved behind the scenes. For example, to update a user's email address, you could use a query like: `UPDATE users SET email = 'newemail@example.com' WHERE user_id = 456`. Similarly, deleting data is just as easy—say goodbye to that outdated user record with a simple `DELETE` statement. SQL makes data manipulation both powerful and straightforward, giving you full control over the data stored in your databases.

As with any powerful tool, SQL requires a bit of practice to master. But don't worry—like learning to ride a bike or master a video game, once you get the hang of it, SQL will become second nature. And the best part? As you become more proficient, you'll be able to tackle increasingly complex problems. Want to calculate the average order value for customers who have made more than 10 purchases? SQL can do that. Need to find out which products are the most popular during specific seasons? SQL can do that too. As you progress, you'll unlock new features of SQL, like subqueries, window functions, and stored procedures, which let you tackle even more advanced challenges. The more you practice, the more powerful your SQL skills become—eventually, you'll be a database wizard capable of solving even the trickiest data problems.

At the heart of SQL's popularity is its versatility. SQL is used by developers, data analysts, data scientists, business analysts, and even marketing teams. It doesn't matter if you're building an e-commerce platform, analyzing customer behavior, or simply maintaining a simple inventory system—SQL is your go-to tool. And because SQL is used by so many people across various industries, learning it opens up a wealth of career opportunities. From creating and managing databases to building complex reporting systems, the demand for SQL knowledge is high. Companies of all sizes rely on SQL to manage and query their data, and those who are proficient in SQL are highly valued in the job market.

SQL's universality doesn't end with its ability to work across various industries; it also works with many different database systems. Whether you're using MySQL, PostgreSQL, Microsoft SQL Server, or even SQLite, the core principles of SQL remain the same. Sure, each system might have its own quirks and additional features, but the fundamentals of SQL are universally applicable. In fact, once you learn SQL on one platform, it's relatively easy to transfer those skills to another. It's like learning to drive a car—once you've mastered the basic mechanics, you can drive virtually any model.

Despite all its power and flexibility, SQL is still evolving. New versions of database systems are constantly being released with additional features and capabilities. For instance, SQL Server has added support for advanced analytics, while MySQL has improved its handling of JSON data. In the future, we can expect more innovations in SQL's capabilities, particularly in the realm of cloud databases and big data. But fear not—while SQL evolves, its core principles remain timeless. As long as you understand the basics, you'll be able to keep up with new trends and features without losing your way.

In conclusion, SQL is the backbone of modern data management. It's simple, powerful, and essential for anyone working with data. Whether you're building a personal project or working for a massive enterprise, knowing SQL will allow you to efficiently store, retrieve, and manipulate your data. By the end of this book, you'll have the knowledge and skills to tackle any SQL challenge that comes your way. So, grab your favorite database system, fire up your SQL client, and let's get started. With the right mindset and some practice, you'll be a SQL master in no time. And who knows, you might just have a little fun along the way!

In the world of technology, databases are a silent force that powers everything. They're not glamorous, they don't make headlines, but without them, the internet as we know it would collapse. Your favorite social media platforms? A well-oiled machine driven by databases. E-commerce sites with millions of products and user reviews? You guessed it: databases. Financial institutions keeping track of trillions of dollars in transactions? Yep, you've got it. And the tool that makes all of this possible is SQL. It's the conductor of this complex orchestra, ensuring that data flows where it's needed, when it's needed, and how it's needed. Just like a skilled musician reading sheet music, SQL allows us to "read" and manipulate the data efficiently and effectively.

However, the journey with SQL doesn't end once you learn the basics of querying and modifying data. A true SQL master knows that databases are not just about asking questions and getting answers—they are about optimization, scaling, and ensuring that everything runs smoothly. Imagine having a database with millions of records, all tightly connected through complex relationships. Without optimization, running queries on that data would be like searching for a needle in a haystack. SQL lets us design queries and structures in such a way that even the largest and most complicated data sets can be handled with ease. You'll learn how to tune your SQL to be as efficient as possible, ensuring that it doesn't just get the job done—it does so quickly and without wasting resources.

One aspect of optimization comes through the use of indexing. Think of an index as a cheat sheet for your database. Just like how the index of a book helps you quickly find a specific chapter or section, an index in a database allows SQL to quickly locate the data you're searching for. Without indexes, every search would require scanning the entire database, a time-consuming and inefficient process. With indexes in place, SQL can jump straight to the right spot in a fraction of the time. But like all tools, indexes must be used wisely. Too many indexes can slow things down as the database must also maintain them, so understanding how and when to use indexes is a crucial part of being a SQL expert.

Now, let's take a quick detour into the world of relational databases versus non-relational (NoSQL) databases. You've probably heard both terms tossed around like they're interchangeable, but they're quite different. Relational databases are built on the concept of tables, and SQL is the language that powers these databases. In contrast, NoSQL databases—like MongoDB, Cassandra, or Couchbase—are designed for handling unstructured or semi-structured data and often don't rely on SQL. NoSQL databases can be extremely useful for certain types of applications, like real-time big data analytics or applications that need flexibility in data modeling. But for traditional, structured data storage and complex queries, relational databases with SQL are still the gold standard. Both have their places in the world of data, and as a SQL master, it's important to know when to choose one over the other.

This chapter wouldn't be complete without a nod to the role that SQL plays in the context of modern applications. Today, many applications rely on databases not only to store information but to provide business logic, facilitate decision-making, and integrate with other systems. For instance, a modern e-commerce platform might use SQL to track inventory levels, process orders, and generate product recommendations based on previous customer behavior. SQL also plays a key role in supporting analytical functions, where it helps process large datasets to uncover trends and insights. Data science and machine learning applications rely on SQL for preprocessing data before it's fed into complex algorithms. So, mastering SQL opens the door to a wide range of fields—from web development to data analysis and even artificial intelligence.

Another vital aspect of databases is data integrity. Imagine if your online store's order system started randomly deleting customer information. Not great, right? SQL helps maintain data integrity by ensuring that the data stored in your database is accurate, consistent, and reliable. With features like transactions, constraints, and triggers, SQL allows you to define rules that preserve data quality. For example, a constraint might ensure that a customer's email address is unique, so two customers don't accidentally share the same address. Transactions allow you to perform multiple actions as a single unit—either all the changes happen, or none of them do. It's like a safety net for data, ensuring that everything stays intact, even in the event of unexpected errors.

As you work your way through this book, you'll also learn how to handle more complex database design concepts, such as normalization and denormalization. Normalization is the process of organizing your data to reduce redundancy and avoid potential pitfalls like update anomalies. Denormalization, on the other hand, is the process of intentionally introducing redundancy to improve query performance. It might seem counterintuitive at first, but denormalization is often used in situations where reading data quickly is more important than maintaining the purest structure. Knowing when and how to apply these concepts is an advanced skill that will separate you from the average SQL user and put you on the path to database wizardry.

Speaking of advanced topics, let's talk about scalability. At some point, the small database you've created for your side project is going to grow into something much larger. When that happens, you'll need to think about scaling your database. SQL offers a variety of strategies to ensure your database can handle increased traffic and data volume, such as partitioning, clustering, and replication. These methods help distribute the load across multiple servers, improve fault tolerance, and ensure that your system remains responsive even as it grows. Understanding how to scale your SQL infrastructure will become crucial as you progress in your database journey, especially if you find yourself working with enterprise-level applications.

One common misconception about SQL is that it's just a tool for developers. Sure, developers use SQL all the time to write applications, but it's not exclusively for them. Data analysts, business analysts, and even project managers benefit from knowing SQL. For example, if you work in a marketing department, you could use SQL to query customer data and gain insights that will help you tailor your campaigns. If you're a product manager, SQL can help you analyze usage data and identify trends that inform your decision-making process. Learning SQL isn't just about writing code—it's about developing a deeper understanding of how data works, how to access it, and how to use it to make smarter decisions.

In conclusion, SQL is the backbone of database management and an essential skill for anyone working with data. It's not just about retrieving records from a database—SQL empowers you to interact with, manipulate, and analyze data in ways that can drive business decisions, improve applications, and fuel innovation. In this chapter, we've covered the fundamental concepts of SQL and databases, from the basics of what a database is to the powerful tools that SQL offers for working with data. As we move through the book, we'll dive deeper into the intricacies of SQL, exploring more advanced topics like indexing, optimization, and security. By the end of this book, you'll not only understand how to use SQL to query and manipulate data—you'll be a true SQL wizard, ready to tackle any data challenge that comes your way. So, let's roll up our sleeves, grab our wands (or, you know, keyboards), and get started with mastering SQL.

Chapter 2: Setting Up Your SQL Environment

Before diving headfirst into SQL queries and database wizardry, it's time to roll up our sleeves and set up the environment where all the magic will happen. This is like preparing your digital workstation—think of it as making sure your desk is organized before you start writing the next great novel, except here, instead of pens and paper, we're using databases and SQL servers. Getting your SQL environment up and running is the first step in the adventure, and trust me, it's easier than it sounds. In this chapter, we'll walk through everything from installing SQL Server to connecting to your database so you can start working with data right away. Whether you're using MySQL, PostgreSQL, or Microsoft SQL Server, the setup process is remarkably similar, and we'll cover all the bases.

Let's begin with a critical question: Which SQL database should you choose? There are several popular options, and the right one for you depends on your needs. MySQL is widely used, especially in web development, and it's known for being lightweight and fast. PostgreSQL, on the other hand, is often praised for its advanced features and standards compliance, making it a favorite for data-driven applications. And then there's Microsoft SQL Server, which is popular in enterprise environments and comes with a suite of additional tools for database management. If you're just starting out, MySQL and PostgreSQL are great choices, but don't worry—we'll cover setup for all three in this chapter. It's like picking your sword before heading into battle: once you're equipped, you'll be ready to conquer data.

Step one is installing your chosen SQL database. If you're using MySQL, head to the official website (https://dev.mysql.com/downloads/). From there, you'll be able to download the installer for your operating system. MySQL provides an installer for Windows, macOS, and Linux, and it's as simple as following a few prompts. The MySQL installer is great because it includes everything you need—server, client, and tools like MySQL Workbench, which is a graphical interface that makes querying easier (and let's be honest, cooler). PostgreSQL has a similar setup process, which you can download from https://www.postgresql.org/download/. The installation wizard will guide you through the process, and before you know it, you'll be ready to fire up the database. For Microsoft SQL Server, you can download the free version, SQL Server Express, from https://www.microsoft.com/en-us/sql-server/sql-server-downloads. This version is perfect for getting started, and the setup process is just as straightforward.

Once you've chosen and downloaded your SQL database, the installation process will usually involve a few simple steps. Follow the installer's instructions, which will typically ask you where you'd like to install the database, whether you want to enable certain features (like security and authentication settings), and how you want to configure things. Don't worry if you don't understand all the options immediately—you can always stick to the default settings and dive into the more complex configurations later. The key here is to get everything set up so you have a working database instance where you can start experimenting with queries and data. Think of this as setting up your first workshop before crafting your masterpiece.

Once the installation is complete, it's time to connect to the database. This is where the magic starts to happen. Each SQL database has its own management tools, and we'll focus on the most common ones for each database. MySQL users will use MySQL Workbench, a slick tool that lets you interact with your database visually. PostgreSQL users have pgAdmin, which is a similar tool that provides a web-based interface for managing the database. Microsoft SQL Server has SQL Server Management Studio (SSMS), which is a comprehensive tool for database management and query execution. These tools provide an easy way to connect to your local or remote SQL database and start running queries without needing to memorize all the command-line options (though we'll get to that soon enough, don't worry).

Connecting to your database through these tools usually requires a few key pieces of information: the database server (typically "localhost" if you're running the server on your local machine), the username (often "root" for MySQL or "postgres" for PostgreSQL), and the password you set during installation. Once you enter these details and hit "connect," you're officially in. It's like unlocking the door to a brand new realm where you can start exploring and manipulating data with nothing more than the power of SQL at your fingertips.

In case you prefer the command line, SQL databases also offer command-line clients that allow you to run queries directly from your terminal or command prompt. If you're using MySQL, you can connect via the `mysql` command; for PostgreSQL, you'd use `psql`; and for SQL Server, there's the `sqlcmd` utility. These tools are powerful, and once you're comfortable with them, you'll feel like a real database ninja. But for now, we'll stick with the graphical tools for ease of use, and we'll dive into the command line later on in the book.

Now that you're connected to your database, let's take a look around. Most SQL management tools come with an interface that allows you to browse your databases, tables, and records. You can explore the structure of your database by expanding the various nodes in the management console. You'll see tables listed in a directory-like format, and inside each table, you'll find columns (the data fields) and rows (the records). This is your playground—a space where you can run queries, modify data, and generally cause all sorts of digital mischief. You're not just a visitor here; you're the data wizard in control.

If you're working with MySQL, you'll also have access to a "Schema" section in MySQL Workbench, where you can create and manage databases. In PostgreSQL, you'll find similar functionality in pgAdmin. Creating a new database is easy—just right-click on the "Databases" node, choose "Create," and voila! You've got yourself a brand-new database. You can also create tables and define the columns that each table will contain. In SQL Server Management Studio, the process is similar, and you can do everything from creating new databases to writing advanced queries—all from the same interface.

As you begin to explore your database, it's essential to get comfortable with some basic commands. First, let's create a table. In MySQL, you might execute the following SQL command:

```
CREATE TABLE customers (id INT PRIMARY KEY, name
VARCHAR(100), email VARCHAR(100));
```

This creates a table named `customers` with three columns: `id`, `name`, and `email`. In PostgreSQL, the syntax is the same. And in SQL Server, it's nearly identical. These commands will create the skeleton of your database where your data will live. It's like creating a set of shelves in your workshop, ready to be filled with the tools (data) you'll need for your project.

If you want to get even fancier, you can define data types for each column to ensure the data is stored properly. For example, `INT` is used for integers, `VARCHAR(100)` is for strings (text), and `DATE` is used for date values. SQL allows you to enforce rules for how data is stored—like requiring an email address to be unique, or making sure a customer's ID is always present. This is part of the data integrity aspect of SQL, which we'll dive deeper into in later chapters. But for now, focus on creating a simple table to get your feet wet.

One more thing to keep in mind as you're setting up your environment is the importance of backups. No one likes to think about losing data, but trust me, it's always better to be safe than sorry. Many SQL database systems come with built-in tools for creating backups of your databases. It's a good habit to back up your work regularly, especially when you're experimenting and learning. After all, we wouldn't want to lose all our hard-earned progress just because we made a little mistake while running a query. It's like taking a screenshot of your work before making any drastic changes—just in case you need to undo something later.

In conclusion, setting up your SQL environment is the first critical step on your journey to becoming a database master. Whether you're using MySQL, PostgreSQL, or SQL Server, the process is simple and straightforward. Once your environment is up and running, you can begin interacting with your data, creating tables, and running queries. But setting up your environment is just the beginning. In the next chapter, we'll dive into the basics of SQL syntax and start writing our first queries. So, fire up your SQL client, and let's get ready to explore the wonderful world of data manipulation! With your environment set up, you're officially ready to begin your SQL adventure. Happy querying!

Alright, now that you've got your SQL environment set up and ready to go, you're no longer just a digital wanderer—you're a database explorer with tools in hand, eager to dig deep into the world of data. But don't get too comfortable just yet; there are a few more important things to keep in mind as you embark on this SQL adventure. After all, a proper setup doesn't just stop at getting the software installed and running. There are some critical configurations and best practices that can save you time, headaches, and even the occasional database disaster down the road.

Let's start with the basics of database security. While it's tempting to set up your environment quickly and start writing queries right away, ensuring that your database is secure from the get-go is key. For starters, you'll need to set a strong password for your database user accounts. Many SQL installations come with a default username (like "root" for MySQL or "postgres" for PostgreSQL), and these default accounts are notorious for being insecure if left unchanged. Make sure to replace these with your own credentials. A good rule of thumb is to use a password that's at least 12 characters long, mixing letters, numbers, and special symbols. It's the digital equivalent of locking your front door—don't leave your data wide open for the taking.

But the setup isn't just about securing passwords. You should also consider limiting user permissions. SQL databases allow you to define who can access certain databases or tables, and at what level. For instance, you might have a "read-only" user who can only view data but can't modify anything, or an "admin" user who has full control. If you're working in a team environment, it's especially important to set up different access levels based on roles, ensuring that users only have access to what they need. This is crucial not only for protecting sensitive data but also for preventing accidental changes or deletions of important records. After all, no one wants to be responsible for deleting an entire table of customer orders because they clicked the wrong button.

Next, let's talk about database maintenance. Setting up your SQL environment isn't just a one-time task. To keep things running smoothly, you'll need to regularly perform maintenance tasks like updating your database software, checking for security patches, and optimizing your queries. Most database systems, including MySQL, PostgreSQL, and SQL Server, release updates that include important fixes, performance improvements, and security enhancements. Keeping your system up to date ensures that you're working with the latest features and that your database is as secure as possible. Most systems allow you to configure automatic updates, which is a great option if you don't want to manually check for new versions every month.

In addition to software updates, database optimization is essential for keeping things running at peak performance. Over time, as data grows and queries become more complex, performance can degrade. This is where tools like indexing come into play. You might be asking, "What's indexing, and why should I care?" Well, imagine trying to find a specific chapter in a book without an index. You'd have to flip through every page—tedious and inefficient, right? Indexing works in much the same way by helping your database quickly find the data you need, without scanning the entire table. It's an essential tool for speeding up query performance, and as your database grows, it will become your best friend.

As you continue to work with SQL, you'll also want to set up a backup strategy. Backups are your safety net. In the world of data management, disasters happen. Whether it's accidental deletion, a failed update, or some other unforeseen calamity, having a backup of your data means you won't lose everything. Most database systems allow you to schedule automatic backups, ensuring that even if something goes wrong, you have a recent snapshot of your data to restore from. Setting up regular backups, especially before making any major changes to your database, is a best practice that cannot be overstated. Trust me—future-you will thank present-you when a database disaster strikes, and all you have to do is restore from your backup.

Let's take a moment to appreciate the beauty of cloud databases. While local setups are fantastic for learning and development, as your projects scale, you may want to explore cloud-based database solutions like Amazon RDS, Google Cloud SQL, or Azure SQL Database. These platforms offer the advantage of automatic backups, scalability, and high availability. They also handle many of the maintenance tasks for you, such as patching and security updates, which frees you up to focus on writing queries and building your applications. Cloud databases come with their own learning curve, but once you're familiar with the basics of SQL, transitioning to the cloud is a logical next step.

Another important concept to understand as you set up your SQL environment is the idea of database migrations. As your database schema evolves over time—adding new tables, changing column types, or adding constraints—you'll need a way to manage these changes. This is especially true in development teams where multiple people are working on the same project. Database migrations are scripts that allow you to apply changes to your database in a controlled, versioned manner. Many modern frameworks and tools (like Django for Python or Rails for Ruby) include built-in migration systems to help automate this process. Understanding how to write and apply migrations ensures that you don't accidentally break things while making updates to your database schema.

Let's not forget about database monitoring. As you start running queries and interacting with your database, it's important to keep an eye on how it's performing. Monitoring tools can help you track things like query performance, memory usage, and disk space. Many database management systems, including MySQL, PostgreSQL, and SQL Server, offer built-in performance monitoring tools that allow you to keep tabs on how efficiently your queries are running. If you notice that certain queries are taking longer than expected, it might be a sign that you need to optimize them, perhaps by adding indexes or rewriting them to be more efficient. Regular monitoring helps you stay on top of your database's health and prevents problems before they escalate.

Now that you've got your environment set up and you're armed with a few maintenance tips, it's time to start working with data. In the coming chapters, we'll dive into the core of SQL itself—how to write basic queries, retrieve data, modify records, and interact with your database like a pro. But before we get to that, take a moment to familiarize yourself with the SQL client or management tool you're using. Open it up, play around a bit, and make sure you're comfortable navigating the interface. Familiarity with your tools will help you feel more confident as you dive deeper into the world of SQL.

As you continue your SQL journey, remember that setup is just the beginning. You've laid the groundwork, but there's so much more to explore and learn. The more you practice and experiment with your database, the more comfortable you'll become. Soon enough, you'll be querying data with ease, optimizing performance, and running sophisticated analyses. In the next chapter, we'll begin our SQL quest in earnest by diving into the basics of SQL syntax. So, get ready to fire up your database, and let's start writing some queries! Happy coding!

Chapter 3: First Steps: The Basic SQL Syntax

Now that your SQL environment is all set up, it's time to roll up our sleeves and dive into the fun part—writing some SQL queries! Think of this chapter as your first taste of the SQL universe, where we'll start with the building blocks and lay a solid foundation for everything that comes next. Writing SQL queries is a bit like crafting a recipe: you need the right ingredients (keywords) and instructions (syntax) to create something delicious (or, in this case, useful). Don't worry, though; SQL syntax isn't as intimidating as it may seem at first. In fact, once you get the hang of it, you'll find that querying databases is surprisingly intuitive—like learning to read a simple, elegant language where your commands are direct and to the point. Grab your virtual pen and paper, because it's time to start writing!

The first thing to understand about SQL syntax is that it's very much based on plain English. You don't need to memorize a complex set of symbols or cryptic commands—just follow the logic of the statement. SQL commands are constructed using simple keywords that are used to tell the database what to do. For example, the most common SQL statement is the **SELECT** statement, which is used to query and retrieve data from a database. Think of it as asking your database, "Hey, what's in this table?" The basic syntax looks like this:

```
SELECT column1, column2 FROM table_name;
```

This command tells the database to return data from the specified columns in the specified table. Easy, right? Let's break it down further: **SELECT** is the keyword that specifies you want to retrieve data. `column1, column2` is a list of the columns you want to retrieve, and **FROM** `table_name` tells SQL which table to pull the data from. Simple, yet powerful!

But what if you don't need all the columns in the table? Maybe you just want to see the names of customers in your database. No problem! You can specify exactly which columns to pull by listing them after the **SELECT** keyword. For example:

```
SELECT first_name, last_name FROM customers;
```

This command will retrieve just the first and last names of all the customers from the `customers` table. The beauty of SQL is that it lets you be as specific as you need. Want to retrieve just one column? No problem. Need multiple columns? Go ahead. It's all up to you. Just keep in mind that if you want to grab every single column in a table (for when you're feeling ambitious), you can use the asterisk (`*`), which acts as a wildcard. For example:

```
SELECT * FROM customers;
```

This will return every column from the `customers` table. But proceed with caution—sometimes all that data can be overwhelming, and in larger tables, it can slow things down. When in doubt, always select only the columns you need.

Alright, we're getting the hang of SELECT statements, but we can take things a step further. SQL is like a digital detective: it allows you to ask very specific questions about the data. To filter your results, you can use the WHERE clause. This acts like a filter, ensuring that only the rows that meet certain conditions are returned. For instance, let's say you want to retrieve the names of customers who live in New York. You can do so by adding a WHERE clause like this:

```
SELECT first_name, last_name FROM customers WHERE city =
'New York';
```

In this case, the database will only return customers who live in New York, because the WHERE clause limits the results to those records that match the condition. You can also use operators like =, >, <, >=, and <= to create more advanced filtering conditions. You can even combine multiple conditions using AND or OR. For example:

```
SELECT first_name, last_name FROM customers WHERE city =
'New York' AND age > 30;
```

This query will return the first and last names of customers who live in New York and are older than 30. It's like asking your database, "Show me only the customers who meet both of these conditions." Pretty handy, right?

Now, let's talk about sorting. Sometimes, you want to order the results of your query. SQL has a simple way to do this using the ORDER BY clause. By default, SQL returns results in no particular order, which might be fine for small datasets but can be chaotic for larger ones. With ORDER BY, you can sort the data either in ascending (ASC) or descending (DESC) order. For example, if you want to see the list of customers ordered by their last name in alphabetical order, you would write:

```
SELECT first_name, last_name FROM customers ORDER BY
last_name ASC;
```

This will return the customers in alphabetical order, from A to Z. If you want to reverse the order and show them from Z to A, just change ASC to DESC. You can also sort by multiple columns. For example:

```
SELECT first_name, last_name, age FROM customers ORDER BY
last_name ASC, first_name ASC;
```

This will sort the customers by last name first and, if two customers share the same last name, it will then sort by their first name. It's like organizing a bookshelf: first by title (last name) and then by author (first name).

Let's take things up a notch by introducing the concept of aggregation. Sometimes, you don't just want to retrieve data—you want to summarize it. SQL gives you several built-in functions to help with this. For instance, the COUNT() function can be used to count the number of rows in a table or the number of times a particular condition is met. Let's say you want to know how many customers live in New York. You can write:

```
SELECT COUNT(*) FROM customers WHERE city = 'New York';
```

This will return a single number representing how many customers live in New York. You can also use other aggregation functions like SUM(), AVG(), MIN(), and MAX() to perform calculations on numeric data. For example, to find the average age of customers:

```
SELECT AVG(age) FROM customers;
```

These aggregation functions are incredibly useful when you need to generate reports or analyze data at a higher level.

Another powerful feature of SQL is the ability to group data together using the GROUP BY clause. This is particularly useful when working with aggregated data. Let's say you want to know how many customers there are in each city. Instead of counting all the customers in the entire table, you can group them by their city:

```
SELECT city, COUNT(*) FROM customers GROUP BY city;
```

This query will return a list of cities along with the number of customers in each one. Grouping is great for breaking down your data into more digestible chunks and seeing patterns emerge.

As we move forward, it's also essential to learn how to combine different types of SQL operations. For example, imagine you need to find out which products were sold in each region during the last quarter. This could involve several tables, one for sales, another for products, and yet another for regions. To pull this all together, you'd need to use a **join**—an advanced yet incredibly powerful concept that allows you to combine data from two or more tables based on related columns. We'll cover joins in more detail later, but for now, understand that SQL's power lies in its ability to combine and manipulate data from multiple sources at once. It's like playing an intricate game of chess where each piece moves strategically to reveal a winning move.

At this point, you've learned some of the fundamental building blocks of SQL: selecting data, filtering it, sorting it, and performing calculations on it. As you grow more comfortable with these basic operations, you'll find that SQL is an incredibly versatile tool for querying, analyzing, and manipulating data. And the best part? These fundamental concepts apply no matter which database system you're using, so once you master them, you're ready to work with any database out there.

Now that you've dipped your toes into the basics of SQL syntax, don't stop here—keep practicing! Try running some queries on your own database, experimenting with different filters, sorting options, and aggregations. The more you practice, the more fluent you'll become in the language of SQL. In the next chapter, we'll dive deeper into even more advanced techniques, like joins and subqueries, that will allow you to work with more complex data structures. But for now, take some time to play around with the queries we've covered so far. Happy querying!

Alright, let's take a quick moment to reflect on the magic we've already uncovered. At this point, you're equipped with the essential skills to write basic SQL queries. You know how to pull specific columns from tables using the **SELECT** keyword, how to filter those results with the **WHERE** clause, and how to sort and group data to find useful insights. But SQL is more than just a series of simple commands—it's a language that opens the door to deeper data exploration. Now that you've gotten comfortable with the basics, let's kick it up a notch by introducing some additional features of SQL syntax that will allow you to handle more complex tasks.

One important concept you'll encounter often is the **LIMIT** clause (or **TOP** in SQL Server). Sometimes, you don't need all the data that matches your query; you just need a sample, or the first few rows that meet your criteria. This is where **LIMIT** (MySQL and PostgreSQL) or **TOP** (SQL Server) comes into play. It's like saying, "Give me just a handful of results from this giant list, please!" For example, let's say you want to see the top 5 customers who made the most purchases. In MySQL or PostgreSQL, the query would look like:

```
SELECT customer_id, SUM(amount_spent) FROM orders GROUP BY
customer_id ORDER BY SUM(amount_spent) DESC LIMIT 5;
```

This will give you the top 5 customers based on how much they've spent. If you're using SQL Server, you'd write:

```
SELECT TOP 5 customer_id, SUM(amount_spent) FROM orders
GROUP BY customer_id ORDER BY SUM(amount_spent) DESC;
```

This clause helps to refine your queries and avoid returning unnecessary rows, which is especially important when working with large datasets.

Another handy tool in SQL is the **DISTINCT** keyword. This is used to eliminate duplicate rows from your query results. Imagine you have a list of customers, and some customers appear multiple times because they've placed several orders. If you just want to see the unique list of customers, you can use `DISTINCT`. For example:

```
SELECT DISTINCT customer_id FROM orders;
```

This will give you a list of each unique customer, regardless of how many times they've ordered. It's a simple but powerful way to make sure your results are clean and free from duplicates. This is like saying, "No repeats, please! I only want one of each."

Let's talk about something even more powerful now: **aliasing**. Aliasing allows you to give temporary, more readable names to tables or columns in your queries, making them easier to work with. For example, let's say you're working with a database that contains a table called `customers`, and you're writing a query that uses the `first_name` and `last_name` columns. Instead of repeatedly writing out `customers.first_name`, you can give the table an alias, like this:

```
SELECT c.first_name, c.last_name FROM customers AS c;
```

Now, you only need to type `c` instead of `customers` every time. This makes your queries shorter and easier to read, especially when you're working with complex joins or long table names. Aliases can also be used with columns. For example, you could rename the `first_name` column to just `name` in the results:

```
SELECT first_name AS name, last_name FROM customers;
```

This will return a column labeled `name` in the output, making the results more user-friendly. Aliasing is one of those little tricks that, once you master it, will make your SQL queries much more elegant and efficient.

Speaking of joins—now that we've covered basic SELECT statements, it's time to introduce you to a more advanced but incredibly useful SQL feature: **joins**. A join allows you to combine data from multiple tables into a single result. You'll use joins when you have related data spread across different tables and you want to bring them together in a single query. For example, imagine you have two tables: `customers` and `orders`. The `customers` table contains customer details, and the `orders` table contains information about the purchases made by those customers. To see the customer details along with their order information, you'll need to perform a join.

The most common type of join is the **INNER JOIN**, which returns rows that have matching values in both tables. Here's an example:

```
SELECT customers.first_name, customers.last_name,
orders.order_date FROM customers INNER JOIN orders ON
customers.customer_id = orders.customer_id;
```

This query joins the `customers` and `orders` tables by the `customer_id` column, returning the first name, last name, and order date of all customers who have placed an order.

The INNER JOIN only includes rows where there's a match between the two tables. If a customer has no orders, they won't appear in the results.

In addition to the INNER JOIN, there are other types of joins like the **LEFT JOIN** (or LEFT OUTER JOIN), which returns all rows from the left table (even if there's no match in the right table) and fills in missing values with NULL. For example, if you wanted to get a list of all customers, including those who haven't placed an order, you could write:

```
SELECT customers.first_name, customers.last_name,
orders.order_date FROM customers LEFT JOIN orders ON
customers.customer_id = orders.customer_id;
```

In this case, the query will return all customers, and if a customer hasn't placed any orders, the order_date will be NULL. This type of join is useful when you want to make sure that no data from the left table is excluded.

Using Aggregate Functions with GROUP BY

By now, you've learned how to pull data from one or more tables using SQL. But what if you need to summarize that data? SQL gives you powerful aggregate functions like COUNT(), SUM(), AVG(), MIN(), and MAX() to help you analyze your data. Let's say you want to know the total number of orders placed by each customer. You can use the COUNT() function in combination with the GROUP BY clause to group the data by customer and then count the number of orders for each one:

```
SELECT customer_id, COUNT(order_id) AS total_orders FROM
orders GROUP BY customer_id;
```

This query will return a list of customers along with the total number of orders they've placed. The GROUP BY clause groups the data by customer_id, and then COUNT(order_id) counts the number of orders for each customer.

These aggregate functions become even more useful when combined with filtering. If you want to count only orders that were placed within the last 30 days, you can add a WHERE clause:

```
SELECT customer_id, COUNT(order_id) AS total_orders FROM
orders WHERE order_date > NOW() - INTERVAL 30 DAY GROUP BY
customer_id;
```

This query will return the total number of orders placed by each customer in the last 30 days. Notice how the WHERE clause is applied before the GROUP BY—this ensures that only the data within the specified timeframe is considered for aggregation.

Conclusion: Your SQL Journey Begins Here

At this point, you've learned some of the core elements of SQL syntax that will serve as the foundation for all your future queries. You now know how to select and filter data, sort it, group it, and even perform calculations on it. With these basic tools in your SQL toolbox, you're ready to start querying your own databases, whether it's for a simple project or a more complex application.

But don't stop here. SQL is a vast and powerful language, and what we've covered so far is just the beginning. In the next chapters, we'll dive into even more advanced topics, like working with subqueries, using joins to bring data from multiple tables together, and manipulating data through insertions, updates, and deletions. As you continue your journey, remember that practice makes perfect. The more queries you write, the more confident and proficient you'll become in using SQL to solve real-world problems.

So, take what you've learned here, try running some queries on your own, and explore the depths of your data. The world of SQL is your oyster—go ahead and start cracking it open! Happy querying, and stay tuned for the next chapter, where we'll take your SQL skills to the next level.

Chapter 4: Filtering Data: WHERE Clauses and Operators

Welcome back, SQL adventurer! Now that you've learned how to pull data from a database with SELECT statements, it's time to refine your search abilities. Imagine you're in a massive library, and your goal is to find the perfect book. If you were to scan every single title in the library, it would take forever. But with the power of filtering, you can focus on just the books that fit your criteria, whether it's the ones written by a specific author, or those with a particular genre. That's exactly what the WHERE clause does in SQL—it allows you to filter the data you're pulling from the database, returning only the rows that match certain conditions. So, get ready to learn how to filter and narrow down your queries using the magical powers of WHERE clauses and operators.

Let's start with the basics. The WHERE clause is used to specify a condition for the rows you want to retrieve. It's like setting the rules for a treasure hunt: "Show me all the customers who live in New York" or "Give me all the orders that were placed after January 1st." The syntax for using WHERE is simple. Here's an example:

```
SELECT first_name, last_name, city FROM customers WHERE
city = 'New York';
```

In this query, we're telling SQL to select the first_name, last_name, and city columns from the customers table, but only for those customers whose city is equal to "New York." Pretty straightforward, right? The WHERE clause filters the results so that only the customers living in New York are shown. If no customers match that condition, you'll simply get an empty result set. SQL doesn't get emotional about this, it just works with the data that matches the conditions.

Now, let's take it up a notch. Filtering isn't just limited to simple equality. You can use a variety of comparison operators to refine your search further. These operators include:

- **=** (equals)

- **!= or <>** (not equal)

- **>** (greater than)

- **<** (less than)

- **>=** (greater than or equal to)

- **<=** (less than or equal to)

For example, let's say you want to find all customers who are older than 30 years. You can use the > operator like this:

```
SELECT first_name, last_name, age FROM customers WHERE age
> 30;
```

This query will return all customers whose age is greater than 30. Similarly, if you want to find customers who are exactly 30 or older, you'd use the >= operator:

```
SELECT first_name, last_name, age FROM customers WHERE age
>= 30;
```

These comparison operators give you the flexibility to ask more specific questions, such as "Who are my customers above a certain age?" or "What products are priced under $20?"

But what if you need to filter based on multiple conditions? No problem! SQL has logical operators that allow you to combine multiple conditions within a **WHERE** clause. The most common logical operators are **AND, OR**, and **NOT**. These operators help refine your query even further, giving you more control over your results. Let's look at **AND** first. If you want to find all customers who live in New York *and* are over the age of 30, you can use the **AND** operator:

```
SELECT first_name, last_name, city, age FROM customers
WHERE city = 'New York' AND age > 30;
```

This query will only return customers who satisfy both conditions. If a customer lives in New York but is under 30, or if they're over 30 but live in a different city, they won't appear in the results. It's like setting two conditions for your treasure hunt: "Only show me the treasures in New York, and only the ones older than 30."

On the flip side, if you want to find customers who either live in New York *or* have made a purchase of over $100, you can use the **OR** operator:

```
SELECT first_name, last_name, city, purchase_amount FROM
customers WHERE city = 'New York' OR purchase_amount > 100;
```

In this case, SQL will return customers who meet either of the conditions—whether they live in New York or their purchase amount exceeds $100. The **OR** operator is handy when you want to include rows that meet at least one condition, without requiring both.

And what about **NOT**? The **NOT** operator allows you to exclude rows that meet a certain condition. For example, if you want to find all customers who don't live in New York, you could write:

```
SELECT first_name, last_name, city FROM customers WHERE NOT
city = 'New York';
```

This query will return customers who do *not* live in New York. It's perfect for situations where you want to exclude certain data from your results.

While we're on the topic of exclusion, SQL also allows you to use the `IN` and `NOT IN` operators for even more efficient filtering. These operators allow you to check whether a column's value matches any value in a list. Let's say you want to find all customers who live in either New York, Los Angeles, or Chicago. You can use `IN` like this:

```
SELECT first_name, last_name, city FROM customers WHERE
city IN ('New York', 'Los Angeles', 'Chicago');
```

This will return customers whose city is one of the three specified. It's like saying, "Give me anyone who fits one of these options," making it more concise than writing multiple `OR` conditions.

If you need to exclude specific values from your search, you can use `NOT IN`. For instance, if you want to find all customers who do not live in New York, Los Angeles, or Chicago, the query would look like this:

```
SELECT first_name, last_name, city FROM customers WHERE
city NOT IN ('New York', 'Los Angeles', 'Chicago');
```

This will return customers who live in cities other than the ones listed, excluding the big three. This is a powerful tool for filtering data when you have multiple values you want to include or exclude in your conditions.

Let's not forget about **wildcards**! Sometimes, you don't know the exact value you're looking for, but you have a pattern in mind. This is where the `LIKE` operator comes in handy. The `LIKE` operator allows you to filter data based on patterns in text values. You can use two wildcards with `LIKE`:

- The percent sign (`%`) represents any sequence of characters (including no characters).

- The underscore (`_`) represents a single character.

For example, if you want to find all customers whose first name starts with the letter "J," you can use this query:

```
SELECT first_name, last_name FROM customers WHERE
first_name LIKE 'J%';
```

This will return customers whose first names start with "J" (e.g., "James," "John," "Jessica"). If you want to find all customers whose last names are exactly five letters long, you could write:

```
SELECT first_name, last_name FROM customers WHERE last_name
LIKE '_____';
```

This query will return all customers whose last names contain exactly five characters, regardless of what those characters are.

You can even combine wildcards with other conditions. For example, to find customers whose email address ends with "@gmail.com," you'd write:

```
SELECT first_name, last_name, email FROM customers WHERE
email LIKE '%@gmail.com';
```

The % at the beginning of the string means "any sequence of characters," and the query will return all customers who have a Gmail address.

Finally, there's one more trick in your filtering toolbox: the **BETWEEN** operator. This allows you to filter data within a range of values. It's like saying, "Give me all the customers whose ages are between 20 and 40." Here's an example:

```
SELECT first_name, last_name, age FROM customers WHERE age
BETWEEN 20 AND 40;
```

This query will return all customers whose ages fall within that range, including the endpoints (20 and 40). It's especially useful for numeric data like ages, prices, and dates.

In conclusion, the `WHERE` clause is an incredibly powerful tool in SQL that allows you to filter and refine your data to get exactly what you need. With the help of comparison operators, logical operators, wildcards, and range filters, you can make your queries more specific and insightful. Whether you're looking for customers in a particular city, products within a certain price range, or emails containing specific keywords, SQL makes it easy to get the data that matters most to you.

The more you practice using the `WHERE` clause, the more efficient and accurate your queries will become. In the next chapter, we'll explore sorting and ordering your data, taking your queries from "nice" to "wow!" So, start experimenting with the filters and operators we've covered, and watch how SQL becomes your trusty data detective. Happy querying!

You've now unlocked the full potential of filtering data with the `WHERE` clause. As we've seen, you can refine your results using a wide variety of operators, logical conditions, and wildcards. These tools give you the flexibility to extract exactly the data you need, whether you're searching for customers in a specific city, filtering products by price, or finding entries that match a pattern. But before we close this chapter, let's take a deeper dive into some more advanced filtering techniques that will take your querying skills to the next level.

Filtering with NULL Values

Sometimes, you'll encounter situations where data is missing or undefined. In SQL, this missing or undefined data is represented by `NULL`. Unlike empty strings or zero values, `NULL` represents an absence of data, and it behaves a little differently when filtering. To check for `NULL` values, you can't use the regular comparison operators like = or !=. Instead, SQL provides the `IS NULL` and `IS NOT NULL` conditions.

For example, if you want to find all customers who have no email address listed, you can write:

```
SELECT first_name, last_name, email FROM customers WHERE
email IS NULL;
```

This query will return customers where the `email` field is missing or undefined. On the other hand, if you want to find customers who have provided an email address (i.e., where the `email` is not `NULL`), you'd use:

```
SELECT first_name, last_name, email FROM customers WHERE
email IS NOT NULL;
```
Filtering for NULL values is particularly useful in situations where you need to identify missing or incomplete data, allowing you to clean up your records or spot gaps in your dataset.

Using Regular Expressions with LIKE (Pattern Matching)

While the LIKE operator with wildcards is great for basic pattern matching, SQL also supports more advanced pattern matching through **regular expressions**. Regular expressions, or regex, are powerful tools used to match complex text patterns. However, not all databases support regex directly in SQL. For example, MySQL and PostgreSQL have limited support for regex, while SQL Server supports it through the PATINDEX function. In MySQL and PostgreSQL, you can use the REGEXP or ~ operators to perform pattern matching.

Let's say you want to find customers whose email address contains either "gmail" or "yahoo." In MySQL, you could write:
```
SELECT first_name, last_name, email FROM customers WHERE
email REGEXP 'gmail|yahoo';
```
This query will return customers whose email address contains either "gmail" or "yahoo". The pipe | is used to indicate "or" in regular expressions. For PostgreSQL, the syntax would be slightly different, using ~:
```
SELECT first_name, last_name, email FROM customers WHERE
email ~ 'gmail|yahoo';
```
Regular expressions allow for much more sophisticated matching. For example, you can search for patterns such as "any number of digits," or "any string that starts with a specific letter," making it incredibly useful when you need to apply more detailed filtering to text-based columns.

Using AND, OR, and NOT in Combination

One of the most powerful aspects of the WHERE clause is the ability to combine multiple filtering conditions using AND, OR, and NOT. You can create complex logical expressions to pull exactly the data you need from your tables.

Let's say you want to find customers who either live in New York *or* Chicago, but you only want to include those who have spent more than $500. Here's how you would write it:
```
SELECT first_name, last_name, city, total_spent FROM
customers WHERE (city = 'New York' OR city = 'Chicago') AND
total_spent > 500;
```
The parentheses here are important—they ensure that the OR condition is evaluated before the AND condition. This query will return customers who either live in New York or Chicago and who have spent more than $500.

What if you wanted to exclude customers from New York entirely and only focus on those who spent more than $500? You can use NOT to do this:

```
SELECT first_name, last_name, city, total_spent FROM
customers WHERE NOT city = 'New York' AND total_spent >
500;
```

This query will return customers who don't live in New York and have spent more than $500. The NOT operator makes it easy to exclude specific conditions from your results.

Filtering Dates and Times

Filtering based on date and time is another common use case in SQL queries. If your database has a column that stores dates (like a `date_of_birth` or `order_date`), you can filter records based on a date range. SQL provides several ways to work with date and time values.

Let's say you want to find all orders placed in the last 30 days. You can use SQL's `NOW()` function (which returns the current date and time) along with the `INTERVAL` keyword:

```
SELECT order_id, order_date FROM orders WHERE order_date >
NOW() - INTERVAL 30 DAY;
```

This query will return all orders placed in the past 30 days, relative to the current date.

You can also filter based on a specific date range. If you want to find orders placed between January 1st, 2020, and December 31st, 2020, you can write:

```
SELECT order_id, order_date FROM orders WHERE order_date
BETWEEN '2020-01-01' AND '2020-12-31';
```

The BETWEEN operator is very useful for filtering date ranges, and it includes the boundary values (in this case, both January 1st and December 31st will be included in the result).

Advanced Use of Logical Operators

While AND, OR, and NOT are powerful, there are times when you may want to build more complex conditions with **nested logic**. You can combine multiple logical operators within the same query by nesting them. For example, let's say you want to find customers who either live in New York or Chicago *and* have made a purchase of over $500, but you want to exclude anyone who has placed more than 10 orders. You could write a query like this:

```
SELECT first_name, last_name, city, total_spent,
order_count FROM customers WHERE (city = 'New York' OR city
= 'Chicago') AND total_spent > 500 AND order_count <= 10;
```

By grouping conditions with parentheses and combining them using logical operators, you can build very detailed queries that return precisely the data you need.

Conclusion: Your Power to Filter is Limitless

The WHERE clause is a powerful tool for filtering data, allowing you to pull exactly the records you need from a database. With the ability to combine multiple conditions, use logical operators, filter on date ranges, exclude NULL values, and even use advanced pattern matching with regular expressions, the possibilities are endless. Whether you're working with a simple list of customers or a large and complex data set, you now have the ability to refine your queries and make your searches more efficient and accurate.

As you continue your journey with SQL, remember that filtering is a crucial skill, and the more you practice, the more proficient you'll become at writing sophisticated queries. The next time you find yourself swimming in a sea of data, just pull out your WHERE clause like a trusty map, and let it guide you to the treasure you're looking for.

In the next chapter, we'll explore how to sort and organize your data using the ORDER BY clause. Sorting will help you make sense of large data sets and ensure that you're looking at your results in the most useful way possible. So, keep experimenting with the techniques you've learned here, and get ready to take your SQL skills to the next level! Happy filtering!

Chapter 5: Sorting Data: ORDER BY and LIMIT

1. Welcome back, SQL explorer! You've learned how to retrieve and filter data, but now it's time to take your queries to the next level by organizing and fine-tuning your results. Imagine you're at a concert, and the band is playing an incredible set. Everything is going smoothly until the lead singer asks, "Do you want to hear the top hits first or the fan favorites?" Without a good plan for how to organize the performance, the crowd could be lost in confusion, not knowing when to expect their favorite song. The same thing happens with data: raw information is valuable, but to make sense of it, you need to organize it in a way that makes it easy to understand and analyze. That's where the magic of the ORDER BY and LIMIT clauses comes into play. These two tools will allow you to sort and control how data is presented, making your queries even more powerful.

2. Let's start with the ORDER BY clause. As the name suggests, ORDER BY is used to sort the results of your SQL query in a specific order. By default, SQL doesn't impose any order on the data it returns—it just pulls everything from the database and presents it as-is, like a stack of unordered papers. But often, you want to see your results in a meaningful order. Whether it's sorting customers by their name, or sorting products by price, ORDER BY gives you control over how your data is displayed.

3. The most basic usage of ORDER BY is to sort your results in ascending order. The default sorting order is **ascending** (ASC), meaning the data will be arranged from the lowest to the highest value (alphabetically for text or numerically for numbers). For example, let's say you want to retrieve a list of customers ordered by their last name in alphabetical order. You would write:

```
SELECT first_name, last_name FROM customers ORDER BY
last_name ASC;
```

This query will return all customers, with their last names sorted from A to Z. Notice that the

ASC keyword is optional because it's the default. So, the query could be written as:

```
SELECT first_name, last_name FROM customers ORDER BY
last_name;
```

This query does exactly the same thing—sorting the last names alphabetically in ascending order.

4. But what if you want to reverse the order? Instead of sorting from A to Z, you want Z to A. You can achieve this by using the DESC keyword, which stands for **descending**. Here's how to write a query that sorts customers' last names from Z to A:

```
SELECT first_name, last_name FROM customers ORDER BY
last_name DESC;
```

This will give you the opposite result, with customers ordered from Z to A. The DESC keyword tells SQL to sort the values in descending order, whether they're numbers, dates, or text.

5. Now, let's take things a step further. In real-life scenarios, you often need to sort by more than one column. For example, imagine you have a list of customers, and you want to sort them first by their city (alphabetically), and then by their last name (also alphabetically). You can do this easily with ORDER BY by specifying multiple columns. Here's how:

```
SELECT first_name, last_name, city FROM customers ORDER BY
city ASC, last_name ASC;
```

In this query, SQL will first sort the customers by their city in alphabetical order, and then, within each city, it will sort them by last name, also alphabetically. If two customers share the same city, they will be ordered by their last name, from A to Z.

6. You can even combine ASC and DESC to fine-tune the sorting. Let's say you want to sort customers by city (A to Z), but then sort their purchase amount in descending order (highest to lowest). Here's the query for that:

```
SELECT first_name, last_name, city, total_spent FROM
customers ORDER BY city ASC, total_spent DESC;
```

This query will sort the customers alphabetically by city and, for customers in the same city, will sort them by their spending, from highest to lowest. It's a great way to organize your data when you need multiple layers of sorting to find the exact information you're after.

7. Now that you know how to sort your results, let's take it one step further. What if you don't need to see every single row of data? Imagine you're working with a table of thousands of customer records, but you only want to see the top 5 spenders. Or maybe you want to preview the first 10 products in a catalog without scrolling through hundreds of pages. That's where the LIMIT clause comes in. It allows you to limit the number of rows returned by your query.

8. The syntax for LIMIT is simple:

```
SELECT column1, column2 FROM table_name LIMIT
number_of_rows;
```

For example, if you want to retrieve the first 5 customers from your list, you can use:

```
SELECT first_name, last_name FROM customers LIMIT 5;
```

This query will return only the first 5 customers from the customers table. Notice that the order in which the rows are returned is important—SQL will return the first 5 rows in the order in which they appear in the table, unless you specify a sorting order using ORDER BY. So, if you want to see the top 5 customers based on their total spending, you can write:

```
SELECT first_name, last_name, total_spent FROM customers
ORDER BY total_spent DESC LIMIT 5;
```

This query will return the 5 customers with the highest total spending. By combining ORDER BY with LIMIT, you can get a snapshot of the top performers in any category.

9. Let's say you want to retrieve a larger set of results, but you want to break it up into smaller, more manageable chunks—this is especially useful in applications where you have many rows to display, like product catalogs or search results. You can use the OFFSET keyword in combination with LIMIT to specify which "page" of results to show. The OFFSET value tells SQL how many rows to skip before it starts returning results.

10. For example, let's say you want to retrieve rows 11 through 20 of your customer list. You can combine LIMIT and OFFSET like this:

```
SELECT first_name, last_name FROM customers ORDER BY
last_name ASC LIMIT 10 OFFSET 10;
```

In this case, LIMIT 10 tells SQL to return 10 rows, and OFFSET 10 tells it to skip the first 10 rows. Essentially, you're asking SQL to return the second "page" of results. You can use this method to paginate your results and show only a subset of data at a time. It's like flipping through the pages of a book—each page containing just a handful of records.

11. Once you've mastered the basic usage of ORDER BY and LIMIT, you can start combining them in more complex queries. For example, suppose you want to find the second set of the top 10 highest-spending customers. You can use ORDER BY, LIMIT, and OFFSET together to create a query like this:

```
SELECT first_name, last_name, total_spent FROM customers
ORDER BY total_spent DESC LIMIT 10 OFFSET 10;
```

This query will return customers ranked 11 to 20 based on their spending. By adjusting the OFFSET value, you can paginate through your data, retrieving results in chunks, without ever needing to process the entire dataset at once.

12. In situations where you're dealing with huge datasets, limiting the number of rows returned is an excellent way to ensure your queries perform well and don't overwhelm your system. Let's say you have a database of millions of records, and you're testing out different queries to analyze data. Using LIMIT helps you quickly preview data without waiting for the entire dataset to load. This practice can save you valuable time during the development and testing phases, especially when experimenting with more complex joins or aggregations.

13. For example, if you're running a query to analyze product sales, but you only want to preview the first 10 records, you can write:

```
SELECT product_name, total_sales FROM products ORDER BY
total_sales DESC LIMIT 10;
```

This query returns the top 10 products by sales, and it allows you to quickly get an overview of the data without processing the entire table. Once you're happy with the query, you can remove the `LIMIT` to retrieve the complete dataset for further analysis.

14. By combining `ORDER BY`, `LIMIT`, and `OFFSET`, you have full control over how data is displayed, whether you need to sort, paginate, or preview a subset of results. These tools allow you to manage large datasets effectively and ensure that you're working with the most relevant data for your needs. When used correctly, they enable you to avoid processing unnecessary rows and help you present the data in the most digestible format.

15. Sorting and limiting data are essential skills in SQL, and mastering them will give you the ability to efficiently work with large datasets, analyze trends, and quickly extract the information you need. Whether you're organizing customer records, managing product listings, or analyzing sales performance, `ORDER BY` and `LIMIT` are crucial tools that every SQL expert needs in their arsenal.

16. In the next chapter, we'll dive into more advanced techniques like aggregation and grouping data. These methods will allow you to summarize your results and perform complex calculations, taking your SQL skills to a whole new level. So, keep practicing your sorting and limiting skills, and get ready to start working with aggregate data in the next chapter! Happy querying!

Chapter 5: Sorting Data: ORDER BY and LIMIT

1. Welcome back, SQL explorer! You've learned how to retrieve and filter data, but now it's time to take your queries to the next level by organizing and fine-tuning your results. Imagine you're at a concert, and the band is playing an incredible set. Everything is going smoothly until the lead singer asks, "Do you want to hear the top hits first or the fan favorites?" Without a good plan for how to organize the performance, the crowd could be lost in confusion, not knowing when to expect their favorite song. The same thing happens with data: raw information is valuable, but to make sense of it, you need to organize it in a way that makes it easy to understand and analyze. That's where the magic of the `ORDER BY` and `LIMIT` clauses comes into play. These two tools will allow you to sort and control how data is presented, making your queries even more powerful.

2. Let's start with the `ORDER BY` clause. As the name suggests, `ORDER BY` is used to sort the results of your SQL query in a specific order. By default, SQL doesn't impose any order on the data it returns—it just pulls everything from the database and presents it as-is, like a stack of unordered papers. But often, you want to see your results in a meaningful order. Whether it's sorting customers by their name, or sorting products by price, `ORDER BY` gives you control over how your data is displayed.

3. The most basic usage of `ORDER BY` is to sort your results in ascending order. The default sorting order is **ascending** (`ASC`), meaning the data will be arranged from the lowest to the highest value (alphabetically for text or numerically for numbers). For example, let's say you want to retrieve a list of customers ordered by their last name in alphabetical order. You would write:

```
SELECT first_name, last_name FROM customers ORDER BY
last_name ASC;
```
This query will return all customers, with their last names sorted from A to Z. Notice that the ASC keyword is optional because it's the default. So, the query could be written as:
```
SELECT first_name, last_name FROM customers ORDER BY
last_name;
```
This query does exactly the same thing—sorting the last names alphabetically in ascending order.

4. But what if you want to reverse the order? Instead of sorting from A to Z, you want Z to A. You can achieve this by using the **DESC** keyword, which stands for **descending**. Here's how to write a query that sorts customers' last names from Z to A:
```
SELECT first_name, last_name FROM customers ORDER BY
last_name DESC;
```
This will give you the opposite result, with customers ordered from Z to A. The **DESC** keyword tells SQL to sort the values in descending order, whether they're numbers, dates, or text.

5. Now, let's take things a step further. In real-life scenarios, you often need to sort by more than one column. For example, imagine you have a list of customers, and you want to sort them first by their city (alphabetically), and then by their last name (also alphabetically). You can do this easily with **ORDER BY** by specifying multiple columns. Here's how:
```
SELECT first_name, last_name, city FROM customers ORDER BY
city ASC, last_name ASC;
```
In this query, SQL will first sort the customers by their city in alphabetical order, and then, within each city, it will sort them by last name, also alphabetically. If two customers share the same city, they will be ordered by their last name, from A to Z.

6. You can even combine **ASC** and **DESC** to fine-tune the sorting. Let's say you want to sort customers by city (A to Z), but then sort their purchase amount in descending order (highest to lowest). Here's the query for that:
```
SELECT first_name, last_name, city, total_spent FROM
customers ORDER BY city ASC, total_spent DESC;
```
This query will sort the customers alphabetically by city and, for customers in the same city, will sort them by their spending, from highest to lowest. It's a great way to organize your data when you need multiple layers of sorting to find the exact information you're after.

7. Now that you know how to sort your results, let's take it one step further. What if you don't need to see every single row of data? Imagine you're working with a table of thousands of customer records, but you only want to see the top 5 spenders. Or maybe you want to preview the first 10 products in a catalog without scrolling through hundreds of pages. That's where the **LIMIT** clause comes in. It allows you to limit the number of rows returned by your query.

8. The syntax for **LIMIT** is simple:
```
SELECT column1, column2 FROM table_name LIMIT
number_of_rows;
```

For example, if you want to retrieve the first 5 customers from your list, you can use:

```
SELECT first_name, last_name FROM customers LIMIT 5;
```

This query will return only the first 5 customers from the `customers` table. Notice that the order in which the rows are returned is important—SQL will return the first 5 rows in the order in which they appear in the table, unless you specify a sorting order using `ORDER BY`. So, if you want to see the top 5 customers based on their total spending, you can write:

```
SELECT first_name, last_name, total_spent FROM customers
ORDER BY total_spent DESC LIMIT 5;
```

This query will return the 5 customers with the highest total spending. By combining `ORDER BY` with `LIMIT`, you can get a snapshot of the top performers in any category.

9. Let's say you want to retrieve a larger set of results, but you want to break it up into smaller, more manageable chunks—this is especially useful in applications where you have many rows to display, like product catalogs or search results. You can use the `OFFSET` keyword in combination with `LIMIT` to specify which "page" of results to show. The `OFFSET` value tells SQL how many rows to skip before it starts returning results.

10. For example, let's say you want to retrieve rows 11 through 20 of your customer list. You can combine `LIMIT` and `OFFSET` like this:

```
SELECT first_name, last_name FROM customers ORDER BY
last_name ASC LIMIT 10 OFFSET 10;
```

In this case, `LIMIT 10` tells SQL to return 10 rows, and `OFFSET 10` tells it to skip the first 10 rows. Essentially, you're asking SQL to return the second "page" of results. You can use this method to paginate your results and show only a subset of data at a time. It's like flipping through the pages of a book—each page containing just a handful of records.

11. Once you've mastered the basic usage of `ORDER BY` and `LIMIT`, you can start combining them in more complex queries. For example, suppose you want to find the second set of the top 10 highest-spending customers. You can use `ORDER BY`, `LIMIT`, and `OFFSET` together to create a query like this:

```
SELECT first_name, last_name, total_spent FROM customers
ORDER BY total_spent DESC LIMIT 10 OFFSET 10;
```

This query will return customers ranked 11 to 20 based on their spending. By adjusting the `OFFSET` value, you can paginate through your data, retrieving results in chunks, without ever needing to process the entire dataset at once.

12. In situations where you're dealing with huge datasets, limiting the number of rows returned is an excellent way to ensure your queries perform well and don't overwhelm your system. Let's say you have a database of millions of records, and you're testing out different queries to analyze data. Using `LIMIT` helps you quickly preview data without waiting for the entire dataset to load. This practice can save you valuable time during the development and testing phases, especially when experimenting with more complex joins or aggregations.

13. For example, if you're running a query to analyze product sales, but you only want to preview the first 10 records, you can write:

```
SELECT product_name, total_sales FROM products ORDER BY
total_sales DESC LIMIT 10;
```

This query returns the top 10 products by sales, and it allows you to quickly get an overview of the data without processing the entire table. Once you're happy with the query, you can remove the `LIMIT` to retrieve the complete dataset for further analysis.

14. By combining `ORDER BY`, `LIMIT`, and `OFFSET`, you have full control over how data is displayed, whether you need to sort, paginate, or preview a subset of results. These tools allow you to manage large datasets effectively and ensure that you're working with the most relevant data for your needs. When used correctly, they enable you to avoid processing unnecessary rows and help you present the data in the most digestible format.

15. Sorting and limiting data are essential skills in SQL, and mastering them will give you the ability to efficiently work with large datasets, analyze trends, and quickly extract the information you need. Whether you're organizing customer records, managing product listings, or analyzing sales performance, `ORDER BY` and `LIMIT` are crucial tools that every SQL expert needs in their arsenal.

16. In the next chapter, we'll dive into more advanced techniques like aggregation and grouping data. These methods will allow you to summarize your results and perform complex calculations, taking your SQL skills to a whole new level. So, keep practicing your sorting and limiting skills, and get ready to start working with aggregate data in the next chapter! Happy querying!

17. As you continue to refine your SQL skills, remember that combining `ORDER BY` and `LIMIT` can unlock even more powerful use cases. Imagine you're working with an e-commerce platform, and you need to find the top-selling products by category for a particular time frame. By using `ORDER BY` and `LIMIT` together, you can quickly pull up the best performers from any given period. Not only can you sort them by sales volume, but you can also limit the number of products shown, so you can focus on just the top few. Whether you're interested in the top 5, top 10, or even the top 100 items, these clauses help you extract the most relevant data without needing to sift through the entire product catalog.

18. Another practical scenario where `ORDER BY` and `LIMIT` shine is in building rankings or leaderboards. For example, if you run an online competition or a game that tracks scores, you can use SQL to display the top scorers. You could write a query like this:

```
SELECT player_name, score FROM leaderboard ORDER BY score
DESC LIMIT 10;
```

This will return the top 10 players with the highest scores, sorted in descending order, so you get the highest score first. If you wanted to see the next 10 players in the list, you'd use the `OFFSET` clause, adjusting the number accordingly. This is a fantastic way to display rankings in your applications without overwhelming users with too much data.

19. It's also important to keep performance in mind when using ORDER BY and LIMIT. While these clauses are great for organizing and limiting your query results, remember that sorting large datasets can be resource-intensive. When working with very large tables or complex queries, adding ORDER BY can slow things down. One way to improve performance is to make sure your columns are indexed, especially if you're frequently sorting by those columns. Indexes can drastically speed up the process of sorting, reducing query time and allowing you to get the results faster. So, as you optimize your queries, don't forget the power of indexing.

20. As with most SQL techniques, practice makes perfect. The more you experiment with ORDER BY and LIMIT, the more comfortable you'll become with how they work together. Don't be afraid to try more complex combinations of sorting and limiting, especially when you need to extract specific slices of data or handle large datasets. Whether you're working on a simple project or building a complex application, these two clauses will become your go-to tools for controlling how data is returned, organized, and presented.

21. In the next chapter, we'll explore even more powerful tools for summarizing and analyzing your data, like aggregate functions and grouping with GROUP BY. These will enable you to calculate totals, averages, counts, and much more, on top of the sorting and limiting techniques you've already learned. But for now, experiment with the ORDER BY and LIMIT clauses in your own SQL environment. Play around with different sorting orders, try using LIMIT to paginate your data, and mix in OFFSET to view different subsets of your data. The world of data organization is at your fingertips, and with these tools, you're well on your way to becoming a SQL master.

22. Sorting and limiting are essential building blocks for any data-driven application, whether you're displaying a list of items, generating reports, or creating dashboards. These clauses give you the flexibility to filter out unnecessary data and present only the most relevant, well-organized information. By combining ORDER BY and LIMIT, you can tailor your SQL queries to get exactly what you need. So, whether you're preparing data for a user-facing interface or simply managing a large dataset, these commands will help you get your data in order.

23. And with that, you've covered one of the key aspects of data manipulation in SQL. Sorting and limiting data are indispensable tools for anyone working with databases, and they're the perfect way to start crafting more readable, actionable queries. Next time you're working on a project, try adding a sorting clause to make your results more digestible, or use LIMIT to focus your analysis on just the top performers.

24. So, get ready for the next step in your SQL journey. You've already started working with basic data manipulation, and now you'll learn how to aggregate and group data to uncover deeper insights. We'll explore the powerful functions that allow you to summarize large datasets and calculate key metrics, making your queries even more insightful and impactful. The next chapter will build on everything you've learned so far, so keep practicing and get ready to dive into aggregation! Happy querying!

Chapter 6: Aggregating Data: COUNT, SUM, AVG, MIN, and MAX

1. Welcome back, SQL wizard! By now, you've learned how to retrieve, filter, and organize data, but what if you want to go beyond simple retrieval? What if you need to calculate summaries, totals, or averages from your data? That's where **aggregation** comes in. Aggregating data allows you to group and calculate values like totals, averages, and counts, transforming your data into useful insights. In this chapter, we'll dive into the most commonly used aggregate functions in SQL—COUNT(), SUM(), AVG(), MIN(), and MAX()—and show you how they can help you perform calculations and derive meaningful conclusions from your datasets.

2. Let's start with the most straightforward aggregate function: **COUNT()**. As the name suggests, COUNT() counts the number of rows that match a certain condition. This is incredibly useful when you want to know how many records meet a specific criterion. For example, if you want to find out how many customers have placed an order, you can write:
```
SELECT COUNT(*) FROM orders;
```
This query returns the total number of rows in the orders table. The asterisk (*) means "count all rows." But what if you only want to count customers who have placed more than one order? You can filter this with a WHERE clause:
```
SELECT COUNT(*) FROM orders WHERE customer_id IN (SELECT
customer_id FROM orders GROUP BY customer_id HAVING
COUNT(order_id) > 1);
```
This will return the count of customers who've placed more than one order. The COUNT() function is especially helpful for calculating the number of records that fit certain conditions in your data.

3. Next up, let's talk about **SUM()**. While COUNT() helps you tally the number of records, SUM() lets you add up the values in a specific column. This is perfect for calculating totals, like the total amount spent by all customers or the total number of units sold in an inventory. For example, to calculate the total sales for all orders, you can write:
```
SELECT SUM(total_price) FROM orders;
```
This query will sum the total_price column across all rows in the orders table, returning the total amount of sales. You can also use SUM() with a WHERE clause to calculate totals for specific subsets of data. Let's say you want to calculate the total sales for orders placed after January 1st, 2021:
```
SELECT SUM(total_price) FROM orders WHERE order_date >
'2021-01-01';
```
This will give you the total sales amount for orders placed after that date.

4. Moving on to a more complex scenario, let's explore the **AVG()** function in greater detail. The AVG() function is fantastic when you need to find the average value of a numeric column, such as the average price of a product, the average age of customers, or the average revenue per order. For example, to find the average amount spent per customer, you can write:
```
SELECT customer_id, AVG(total_spent) FROM orders GROUP BY
```

```
customer_id;
```
This query will return the average amount spent by each customer. AVG ( ) is particularly useful when you're working with financial data or any dataset that requires a mean value to summarize the numbers. It's also important to remember that AVG ( ) can be combined with WHERE clauses or even other aggregate functions to refine your analysis.

5. While aggregation functions like COUNT ( ), SUM ( ), and AVG ( ) are powerful, they only give you part of the story when used in isolation. The true power of aggregation shines when you start to combine these functions with grouping and filtering. For example, suppose you want to find out which products have been sold the most in terms of both quantity and total revenue. You can use SUM ( ) for the total revenue and COUNT ( ) for the number of items sold, all grouped by product:
```
SELECT product_id, COUNT(product_id) AS num_sold,
SUM(total_price) AS total_revenue FROM sales GROUP BY
product_id ORDER BY total_revenue DESC;
```
This query will return the products ordered by total revenue, showing both the number of units sold and the total amount generated by those sales. You can easily compare products to see which ones are the best performers in both quantity and revenue. Combining COUNT ( ), SUM ( ), and GROUP BY allows you to get a multi-dimensional view of your data.

6. As you work with aggregates, you may also encounter the **HAVING** clause, which works hand-in-hand with GROUP BY. The HAVING clause allows you to filter groups of records after they've been aggregated. This is different from the WHERE clause, which filters individual rows before aggregation. For instance, if you wanted to find customers who have spent more than $500 in total, you would use HAVING like this:
```
SELECT customer_id, SUM(total_spent) FROM orders GROUP BY
customer_id HAVING SUM(total_spent) > 500;
```
This query will return only customers who have spent more than $500 across all their orders. The HAVING clause comes in handy when you need to filter aggregated data, such as showing only groups that meet a certain threshold.

7. Aggregation functions are also essential when analyzing data over time. For example, suppose you want to find the monthly total sales for a given year. By combining SUM ( ) with the MONTH ( ) function (or its equivalent in your database), you can calculate totals for each month. Here's how you can do that for a sales table:
```
SELECT YEAR(order_date) AS year, MONTH(order_date) AS
month, SUM(total_price) AS monthly_sales FROM orders GROUP
BY YEAR(order_date), MONTH(order_date) ORDER BY year,
month;
```
This query will return the total sales for each month of each year, allowing you to track trends in sales performance over time. You can further customize this query by filtering the results for a particular year or month range using the WHERE clause. Aggregating data by time periods such as days, months, or years is critical for performing trend analysis and forecasting.

8. Let's not forget about **MIN()** and **MAX()**, which provide invaluable insight when you want to find the smallest and largest values in a dataset. For example, if you're analyzing a product catalog and want to know the cheapest and most expensive products, you could write:

```
SELECT MIN(price) AS min_price, MAX(price) AS max_price
FROM products;
```

This query will return the lowest and highest prices in the `products` table. These functions are particularly useful when you're trying to find outliers in your data, whether it's the highest sales amount, the lowest price, or the oldest or newest date. You can also use `MIN()` and `MAX()` in combination with `GROUP BY` to analyze extremes within groups. For example, if you want to know the most expensive and cheapest products in each category, you can write:

```
SELECT category, MIN(price) AS min_price, MAX(price) AS
max_price FROM products GROUP BY category;
```

This will give you the lowest and highest prices within each category, helping you identify pricing trends within different segments of your inventory.

9. One powerful feature of aggregation in SQL is that it can help you find **outliers** or **anomalies** in your data. By using the combination of `COUNT()`, `SUM()`, `AVG()`, `MIN()`, and `MAX()`, you can quickly pinpoint values that deviate from the norm. For example, let's say you're analyzing customer transactions and want to identify customers whose total spending is significantly higher or lower than the average. You can use `AVG()` to find the mean and `MAX()`/`MIN()` to identify customers who have exceeded or fallen below certain thresholds. This can help with tasks like fraud detection, quality control, or identifying your highest-value customers.

10. In conclusion, aggregation in SQL is a fundamental skill that allows you to summarize, analyze, and derive valuable insights from your data. Whether you're counting the number of records, summing totals, calculating averages, or finding the extremes, aggregation is a powerful tool that turns raw data into actionable information. With the ability to group data and filter it with `HAVING`, you can conduct complex analyses to uncover trends and patterns in your datasets. These functions—`COUNT()`, `SUM()`, `AVG()`, `MIN()`, and `MAX()`—are indispensable for anyone working with databases, whether you're in marketing, finance, operations, or any other data-driven field.

11. Now that you've learned how to aggregate data effectively, it's time to practice! Try combining these aggregation functions with `GROUP BY` to explore your datasets and generate insights. For example, analyze the total revenue for each region, calculate the average number of orders per customer, or find the highest-paid employees in your company. The more you experiment with these functions, the more proficient you'll become at summarizing data. Don't hesitate to challenge yourself by creating more complex queries that involve multiple aggregation functions and conditions.

12. Aggregation can be particularly helpful when working with reporting tools or dashboards, where you often need to display summarized data. Many business intelligence (BI) tools rely heavily on aggregate functions to create meaningful visualizations like pie charts, bar graphs, or trend lines. For instance, if you're building a dashboard for sales performance, you may need to display the total sales per month, average sales per product, or maximum order size. SQL's aggregation capabilities make these types of reports quick and easy to generate, ensuring that the data you present is both accurate and insightful.

13. Another point worth mentioning is how SQL allows for flexible data manipulation. You can create complex queries that combine aggregation with other SQL functions like `JOIN`, `WHERE`, and `HAVING`, making it possible to analyze data across multiple tables. For example, you could join customer data with order data, then use `SUM()` to calculate the total revenue per customer, and filter the results to include only those who spent more than $1,000. The power of SQL lies in its ability to work with various types of data and transform it into the precise information you need.

14. As you continue to deepen your understanding of SQL, aggregation will remain one of the most important tools in your data toolkit. It simplifies complex datasets, helping you focus on the insights that matter most. Whether you're preparing reports, analyzing trends, or making business decisions, the ability to aggregate data quickly and efficiently will set you apart as a skilled SQL practitioner. So, as you proceed to the next chapters, remember that aggregation is key to unlocking the value hidden in your data.

15. In the next chapter, we'll build on these aggregation skills by introducing **joins** and **subqueries**. These advanced techniques will allow you to bring together data from multiple tables, making it possible to run even more powerful analyses. With joins, you'll learn how to combine related data from different tables, and subqueries will let you embed one query inside another, enabling even more complex logic. Together, these tools will allow you to work with your data in new and exciting ways. So, keep practicing your aggregation skills, and get ready for the next stage of your SQL journey—there's still so much more to explore! Happy querying!

16. As we close out our exploration of aggregation in SQL, it's worth taking a moment to reflect on how these functions can be applied in real-world scenarios. Aggregation is used across many industries for everything from generating sales reports, calculating customer engagement metrics, identifying trends, and even making business decisions. In a marketing context, for example, you might use `COUNT()` to analyze how many customers have engaged with a campaign, or `SUM()` to tally up campaign spending. In finance, `AVG()` can help determine the average investment return over time, while `MAX()` and `MIN()` can highlight the highest and lowest performing investments.

17. These aggregate functions also become critical when performing data validation and quality checks. For instance, if you're managing customer information, using `COUNT()` can quickly identify if certain customer groups are underrepresented in your dataset. Similarly, `MIN()` and `MAX()` can be used to verify that values like ages or prices fall within expected ranges, helping to ensure the consistency and integrity of your data. Using aggregation, you can perform these sanity checks across multiple dimensions, ensuring your database remains in top form.

18. In addition, aggregation is invaluable when it comes to **data summarization and report generation**. Let's say you're responsible for generating weekly sales reports for your company. Rather than manually calculating totals, averages, and other summary statistics for each region or product line, you can use SQL aggregation functions to quickly summarize the data at the push of a button. By writing a few well-structured SQL queries, you can generate detailed, up-to-date reports that reflect the performance of different aspects of your business. This efficiency is a huge advantage in any industry where timely and accurate information is essential.

19. Another great thing about aggregation is how it allows you to answer complex business questions. For example, imagine you're trying to determine which sales representatives have exceeded their quarterly targets. By using `SUM()` with `GROUP BY`, you can quickly calculate total sales by representative, compare them to their targets, and highlight the top performers. Similarly, you can use `COUNT()` to determine how many customers made repeat purchases or how many orders were placed within a given time frame. Aggregation allows you to sift through enormous amounts of data and extract only the most relevant, high-level insights.

20. It's also important to note that while SQL aggregation is a powerful tool, it's not just about writing basic queries. As you advance in SQL, you'll learn to combine aggregation with more advanced techniques, like joins and subqueries, which let you analyze data across multiple tables. This will allow you to generate even more sophisticated reports, such as finding the total sales for customers who bought products in certain categories or calculating the average spend per region across different periods. These advanced techniques unlock more complex analyses that offer a deeper understanding of your data.

21. As with any tool, it's essential to know when and how to use aggregation. While aggregation functions are incredibly useful, you need to be mindful of performance when working with large datasets. Aggregating large volumes of data without any filtering or optimization can lead to long query times and a negative impact on the overall performance of your database. That's why combining aggregation with effective indexing and query optimization techniques is important. Indexing frequently queried columns or breaking up large queries into smaller, more manageable parts can greatly improve the speed and efficiency of your queries.

22. In practice, aggregation functions are one of the first things that data analysts, data scientists, and even business users learn to master. The ability to quickly and effectively summarize large datasets is crucial in any data-driven profession. With the knowledge of `COUNT()`, `SUM()`, `AVG()`, `MIN()`, and `MAX()`, you now have the ability to start extracting valuable insights from your data. The key is to continue practicing these functions and applying them to different types of data, as real-world datasets tend to be messy and require a bit of creativity to clean and structure them for analysis.

23. To wrap things up, mastering SQL aggregation is like unlocking a superpower for working with data. With the ability to calculate sums, averages, counts, and extremes, you can derive deep insights from your data that are essential for decision-making. Whether you're looking to generate a quick total, analyze sales trends, or break down performance across different categories, these functions will help you manipulate data in powerful ways. As you advance through the book, you'll continue to build on these skills, and soon, you'll be working with more complex SQL queries that tackle even more sophisticated data problems.

24. So, as you take a break from this chapter, try applying these aggregation functions to a dataset you're working with—whether it's an existing project or one of your own making. Test out how `GROUP BY`, `HAVING`, and `COUNT()` can help you make sense of your data, and see how `SUM()`, `AVG()`, `MIN()`, and `MAX()` can give you quick insights into your datasets. With these tools, you'll start to see how data aggregation simplifies complex tasks, making you more efficient and better equipped to analyze any dataset.

25. In the next chapter, we'll tackle even more advanced SQL topics like **joins** and **subqueries**, which will allow you to bring together data from different tables and write more sophisticated queries. These new techniques will enhance your ability to perform even deeper analysis and uncover hidden insights. So, keep practicing your aggregation skills, and get ready to dive into the next chapter—there's plenty more SQL magic ahead. Happy querying, and keep aggregating!

Chapter 7: Joins: Combining Data from Multiple Tables

1. Welcome to one of the most exciting and powerful features in SQL—**joins**! If you've ever worked with databases, you've probably realized that data is often spread across multiple tables. A well-designed database stores related pieces of information in different tables, allowing for efficient organization and management. But how do you pull all that data together when you need it? The answer is SQL joins. Joins allow you to combine data from two or more tables based on a related column, making it possible to perform complex queries and uncover deeper insights. Whether you're pulling customer details along with their orders or retrieving employee information along with their department, joins are your key to linking tables and extracting valuable data.

2. At its core, a join is simply a way to connect rows from two or more tables based on a common column. But before you start thinking this is as easy as pie, let's break it down: there are different types of joins, each used for different purposes. The most common join types are **INNER JOIN**, **LEFT JOIN**, **RIGHT JOIN**, and **FULL JOIN**. Understanding how each one works and when to use them is crucial for combining data in the right way. In this chapter, we'll dive into these join types and provide examples to help you understand how to use them effectively in your SQL queries.

3. Let's start with the most commonly used join—the **INNER JOIN**. An **INNER JOIN** returns only the rows where there is a match in both tables. In other words, it combines records from both tables that share a common value in the specified columns, and excludes rows where no match is found. For example, suppose you have two tables: one for `customers` and another for `orders`. Each order in the `orders` table is associated with a `customer_id` in the `customers` table. To retrieve a list of customers and their orders, you would write:

```
SELECT customers.first_name, customers.last_name, orders.order_id FROM customers INNER JOIN orders ON customers.customer_id = orders.customer_id;
```
This query will return the first and last names of customers along with their associated order IDs,

but only for customers who have placed an order. If a customer doesn't have any orders, they won't appear in the results.

4. The **LEFT JOIN** (or **LEFT OUTER JOIN**) is another common type of join. Unlike the `INNER JOIN`, which only includes rows with matching values in both tables, the `LEFT JOIN` returns all rows from the **left** table and the matching rows from the **right** table. If there's no match in the right table, the query will still return the rows from the left table, but it will fill in the missing values with `NULL`. This is useful when you want to retrieve all records from one table, regardless of whether there's a corresponding record in the other table. Here's an example:

```
SELECT customers.first_name, customers.last_name,
orders.order_id FROM customers LEFT JOIN orders ON
customers.customer_id = orders.customer_id;
```

This query will return a list of customers, along with their order IDs if they have any. Customers who haven't placed an order will still appear in the result, but their `order_id` will be `NULL`. The `LEFT JOIN` is great when you need a complete list from one table, even if there are no corresponding records in the second table.

5. The **RIGHT JOIN** (or **RIGHT OUTER JOIN**) is similar to the `LEFT JOIN`, but it works in the opposite direction. A `RIGHT JOIN` returns all rows from the **right** table and the matching rows from the **left** table. If there's no match in the left table, the query will still return the rows from the right table, filling in missing values with `NULL`. You might use a `RIGHT JOIN` when you want to make sure you get every record from the second table, even if there isn't a corresponding match in the first table. Here's an example:

```
SELECT customers.first_name, customers.last_name,
orders.order_id FROM customers RIGHT JOIN orders ON
customers.customer_id = orders.customer_id;
```

This query will return all the orders from the `orders` table, along with the customer's first and last name. If an order doesn't have a matching customer, the `first_name` and `last_name` will be `NULL`. While `LEFT JOIN` is more common, the `RIGHT JOIN` is useful in specific scenarios where you need to prioritize the right table.

6. A **FULL JOIN** (or **FULL OUTER JOIN**) is the most comprehensive of all the joins. It returns all rows when there's a match in either the left or the right table. If there's no match in one of the tables, the query will still return the row from the other table, with `NULL` values for the columns of the table without a match. This join is useful when you need a complete result that includes all records from both tables, whether they have a matching row or not. For example, let's say you want to get a full list of customers and their orders, including customers who haven't ordered anything and orders that don't have a corresponding customer:

```
SELECT customers.first_name, customers.last_name,
orders.order_id FROM customers FULL JOIN orders ON
customers.customer_id = orders.customer_id;
```

This query will return every customer along with their order ID, and every order along with the corresponding customer information. If a customer hasn't placed an order, their order ID will be

NULL, and if an order doesn't have a matching customer, the customer's name will be NULL. The FULL JOIN is perfect when you need a comprehensive view of two tables, regardless of whether the rows have a match.

7. At this point, we've covered the basics of the main types of joins. But what about when you need to join more than two tables? No problem! SQL lets you chain multiple joins together to combine data from more than two tables. For example, let's say you want to find out which products customers have ordered, along with their order details and the customer information. You can join the customers, orders, and products tables in a single query:

```
SELECT customers.first_name, customers.last_name,
products.product_name, orders.order_id FROM customers INNER
JOIN orders ON customers.customer_id = orders.customer_id
INNER JOIN products ON orders.product_id =
products.product_id;
```
This query retrieves the customer's name, the product they ordered, and the order details by joining three tables—customers, orders, and products—in a chain. You can continue chaining joins together as needed, allowing you to combine data from multiple tables in a single query.

8. When joining multiple tables, it's important to understand how to manage **ambiguous column names**. If two tables have columns with the same name, you'll need to specify which table the column belongs to by using table aliases. For example, let's say both the customers and orders tables have a column named customer_id. To avoid confusion, you can assign aliases to each table:

```
SELECT c.first_name, c.last_name, o.order_id FROM customers
AS c INNER JOIN orders AS o ON c.customer_id =
o.customer_id;
```
In this query, we've given the customers table the alias c and the orders table the alias o, making it clear which table each column belongs to. This ensures that SQL knows exactly which customer_id to use in the join condition.

9. Another key consideration when working with joins is **performance**. Joins, especially with large tables, can be resource-intensive. When you join multiple tables, SQL has to look up matching rows in each table, which can result in slower queries if the tables are large. To improve performance, make sure your tables are properly indexed on the columns used for joining. For example, if you frequently join the customers table on the customer_id column, adding an index to that column can significantly speed up the query. Additionally, try to use joins wisely—don't join unnecessary tables, and always filter your data as much as possible using WHERE or HAVING clauses before performing a join.

10. In conclusion, SQL joins are essential for working with relational databases. They allow you to combine data from multiple tables based on common columns, enabling you to create comprehensive queries and gain deeper insights. Whether you're using INNER JOIN for matching records, LEFT JOIN for including all records from one table, RIGHT JOIN for including all records from another table, or FULL JOIN for getting all records from both, joins make it easy to work with data across different tables. As you advance in SQL, mastering joins will be key to running more complex and meaningful queries. So, practice joining tables in your own database, experiment with different join types, and get ready for even more powerful SQL techniques coming your way!

11. In the next chapter, we'll dive into **subqueries**—another powerful SQL feature that lets you embed one query inside another. Subqueries will help you solve more complex problems and refine your data retrieval strategies. But for now, keep practicing your joins, and start combining data from multiple tables. The more you practice, the more natural joins will become. Happy querying!

12. As we continue exploring joins, it's worth noting that there are **self-joins**, a special case of joining a table to itself. This can be useful when you need to relate rows in the same table to each other. For example, let's say you have an `employees` table where each employee has a manager (also an employee in the same table). To find the employees along with their managers' names, you would perform a self-join. Here's how you can do it:

```
SELECT e.first_name AS employee_name, m.first_name AS manager_name FROM employees e INNER JOIN employees m ON e.manager_id = m.employee_id;
```

In this query, we've aliased the `employees` table as `e` for employees and `m` for managers. The join condition links an employee's `manager_id` to the `employee_id` of their manager, effectively combining rows from the same table. Self-joins are particularly useful for hierarchical data, such as organizational structures or category hierarchies.

13. Another interesting feature of joins is how you can combine them with **aggregate functions** to create complex data analyses. Let's take the example of an online store where you want to analyze the total amount spent by each customer, but you also want to group the data by region. You can use an `INNER JOIN` between the `customers` and `orders` tables and then apply the `SUM()` aggregate function. For instance, here's how to find the total amount spent by customers in each region:

```
SELECT customers.region, SUM(orders.total_price) AS total_spent FROM customers INNER JOIN orders ON customers.customer_id = orders.customer_id GROUP BY customers.region;
```

In this query, we join the `customers` and `orders` tables, and then use `SUM()` to calculate the total amount spent for each region, grouping the results by `region`. This combination of joins and aggregation is an excellent way to summarize and analyze data across different categories or groups.

14. Joins also become incredibly powerful when you start using them with **subqueries**. A subquery allows you to embed one query inside another, enabling you to work with more complex filtering and data retrieval strategies. For example, if you wanted to find customers who have placed more than the average number of orders, you could first calculate the average number of orders in a subquery and then filter the customers based on this value. Here's how that might look:

```
SELECT customer_id, COUNT(order_id) AS total_orders FROM
orders GROUP BY customer_id HAVING COUNT(order_id) >
(SELECT AVG(order_count) FROM (SELECT customer_id,
COUNT(order_id) AS order_count FROM orders GROUP BY
customer_id) AS subquery);
```

This query first calculates the average number of orders in the subquery and then filters the main query to return customers who have placed more than the average number of orders. Subqueries in combination with joins allow you to handle more intricate queries that involve multiple levels of data analysis.

15. When you work with multiple tables, always be mindful of **duplicate data**. Joins can sometimes return duplicate rows if the tables being joined contain repeating values in the columns that are used for matching. To avoid duplicates, you can use the `DISTINCT` keyword to ensure your results only return unique rows. For example, if you want to find a list of unique customers who have placed orders, you can modify your query like this:

```
SELECT DISTINCT customers.first_name, customers.last_name
FROM customers INNER JOIN orders ON customers.customer_id =
orders.customer_id;
```

In this case, `DISTINCT` ensures that you don't get duplicate customer names if a customer has placed multiple orders. This is an important concept to keep in mind when working with joins, especially in tables where there may be repeating values due to the relationships between the data.

16. As with any SQL operation, **performance** is a crucial consideration when working with joins. When joining multiple large tables, SQL has to scan through the records and find matching rows, which can be resource-intensive. To optimize performance, you should ensure that the columns used for joining (such as `customer_id` or `product_id`) are indexed. Indexes allow the database to quickly locate matching rows, significantly speeding up the join operation. Additionally, consider using `INNER JOIN` over `OUTER JOINs` when you don't need all the rows from both tables, as `INNER JOINs` are typically faster.

17. Another way to optimize join performance is by carefully planning the order in which you join tables. When working with complex queries involving multiple joins, start by joining the tables that filter the data the most. This helps reduce the dataset early on, making subsequent joins faster. For example, if you're working with sales data and customer data, and you know there are many more records in the sales table than the customer table, it might make sense to join the smaller `customers` table first and then join the larger `sales` table.

18. Joins also provide a great way to handle **many-to-many relationships** between tables. In these types of relationships, a single row in one table can be related to multiple rows in another table. For example, in a system that tracks books and authors, one book can have multiple authors, and one author can write multiple books. To combine these related tables, you would use a join through an intermediary table. Here's an example of how to query such a relationship:

```
SELECT authors.name, books.title FROM authors INNER JOIN
book_author ON authors.author_id = book_author.author_id
INNER JOIN books ON book_author.book_id = books.book_id;
```

In this case, the `book_author` table acts as the intermediary that links authors and books, allowing you to retrieve the author names along with the titles of the books they've written.

19. Another aspect to consider when working with joins is **data integrity**. Always ensure that the columns you are joining on contain clean, consistent data. If there are nulls, mismatched data types, or other inconsistencies in the columns used for joining, it can lead to incomplete or incorrect results. Regular data cleaning and validation are essential for ensuring that your joins work as expected and return meaningful, accurate results. If you encounter unexpected results during joins, double-check the integrity of the data and consider using functions like `COALESCE()` to handle null values where appropriate.

20. In conclusion, joins are an essential tool for combining data from multiple tables in SQL. They allow you to link tables in meaningful ways, providing you with the flexibility to query complex datasets and uncover valuable insights. Whether you're working with `INNER JOIN`, `LEFT JOIN`, `RIGHT JOIN`, or `FULL JOIN`, understanding how and when to use each type of join will help you solve a wide range of data problems. Joins are especially useful for aggregating data, analyzing trends, and reporting on multi-table datasets.

21. As you continue your journey in SQL, remember that joins are just one part of the puzzle. In the next chapter, we'll dive into **subqueries**—a powerful SQL technique that allows you to embed queries inside other queries. This will enable you to write even more sophisticated queries and perform complex operations that go beyond what you can accomplish with joins alone. So, practice using joins in your SQL queries, and get ready for the next step in your data adventure! Happy querying!

Chapter 8: Subqueries and Nested Queries

1. Welcome to the world of **subqueries** and **nested queries**! By now, you've mastered the basics of SQL, including joins, aggregations, and filtering. But sometimes, the data you need is so complex that you can't achieve your goal with a single, flat query. That's where subqueries and nested queries come in. Subqueries, or "queries within queries," allow you to perform complex data retrieval and calculations by embedding one query inside another. They help you break down a problem into smaller, more manageable pieces, which is a powerful technique when you're dealing with multi-step data analysis. In this chapter, we'll explore the concept of subqueries, learn how to write them, and see how they can help you solve real-world data challenges.

2. A subquery is typically used to return a set of results that can be used by the outer query in a variety of ways. The result of a subquery can be used as a filter in the `WHERE` clause, as a column in the `SELECT` clause, or as a temporary table in the `FROM` clause. One of the key aspects of subqueries is that they allow you to break down complex problems into smaller, more manageable parts. For example, if you need to retrieve records from a table based on calculations done on another table, a subquery lets you perform the necessary computations without needing to create a separate view or table. Let's go through a few examples to explore how subqueries can be applied in different parts of a SQL query.

3. One of the most common places to use subqueries is in the **WHERE** clause. Subqueries in the WHERE clause are often used to filter results based on the outcome of another query. Let's say you have an `orders` table and a `customers` table, and you want to find all customers who have placed an order worth more than $100. Instead of writing complex joins or calculations directly in the WHERE clause, you can write a subquery to first find all customer IDs with large orders and then use that result in your main query. Here's an example:

```
SELECT first_name, last_name FROM customers WHERE
customer_id IN (SELECT customer_id FROM orders WHERE
total_price > 100);
```

In this case, the subquery (`SELECT customer_id FROM orders WHERE total_price > 100`) retrieves all customer IDs who have placed orders worth more than $100. The outer query then uses this list of customer IDs to retrieve their names. The subquery simplifies the logic by isolating the condition for filtering orders.

4. A subquery can also be used in the **SELECT** clause to compute values for each row returned by the outer query. This allows you to perform calculations or transformations on the data as it's being retrieved. For example, imagine you want to list each customer and the number of orders they have placed, but you don't want to use a separate `COUNT()` query. Instead, you can use a subquery in the SELECT clause to calculate the number of orders for each customer. Here's how you might write that:

```
SELECT first_name, last_name, (SELECT COUNT(*) FROM orders
WHERE orders.customer_id = customers.customer_id) AS
order_count FROM customers;
```

In this query, the subquery (`SELECT COUNT(*) FROM orders WHERE orders.customer_id = customers.customer_id`) calculates the number of orders placed by each customer. This result is returned alongside the customer's name, and the subquery runs for each row in the outer query, producing the desired output in a single query.

5. A powerful feature of subqueries is their ability to be used in the **FROM** clause, where the result of the subquery can act as a virtual table or derived table. This is helpful when you need to perform complex filtering or aggregation before the data is processed by the outer query. For example, if you want to find out the total sales per product, but only for products that have been ordered more than 100 times, you can use a subquery in the FROM clause like this:

```
SELECT product_id, total_sales FROM (SELECT product_id,
SUM(total_price) AS total_sales FROM orders GROUP BY
product_id HAVING COUNT(order_id) > 100) AS product_sales;
```

Here, the subquery in the FROM clause calculates the total sales for each product and filters out those products that have fewer than 100 orders. The outer query then uses this temporary result to display the `product_id` and `total_sales`. Using a subquery in the `FROM` clause allows you to prepare and filter your data before any further analysis or aggregation is performed.

6. Another common use of subqueries is for **nested queries**. Nested queries involve embedding a subquery within another subquery, creating a multi-layered query. These can be useful when the results of one subquery are needed to further filter or calculate values in another subquery. For example, let's say you want to find all customers who have placed orders worth more than the average order value. This requires two steps: first, calculating the average order value, and then comparing each customer's total order value to this average. Here's how you might write the query using nested subqueries:

```
SELECT customer_id, first_name, last_name FROM customers
WHERE customer_id IN (SELECT customer_id FROM orders WHERE
total_price > (SELECT AVG(total_price) FROM orders));
```

The innermost subquery (`SELECT AVG(total_price) FROM orders`) calculates the average total price of all orders. The second-level subquery then filters the `orders` table, selecting only those rows where the order price is above the average. Finally, the outer query retrieves the names of the customers whose orders meet this condition. Nested subqueries can become quite complex, but they offer a flexible and powerful way to solve multi-step data problems.

7. As with any tool, there are **performance considerations** when using subqueries. While subqueries are convenient and elegant, they can sometimes be less efficient than other SQL techniques, especially when they involve large datasets. Each subquery in the query must be executed for each row in the outer query, which can lead to slow performance if you're working with large tables. To improve performance, try to use joins instead of subqueries when possible, as joins are typically optimized for better performance in most SQL engines. Additionally, ensure that the columns used in subqueries are indexed, as this can help speed up query execution.

8. Subqueries also have their limitations. They can be difficult to manage in very complex queries, especially when nested multiple times. For example, while they're great for breaking down a problem into smaller steps, deeply nested subqueries can make a query harder to read, debug, and maintain. If you find yourself writing complex nested subqueries frequently, it might be a sign that you should reconsider your database design or consider using **temporary tables** or **views** to store intermediate results. These alternatives can sometimes provide more clarity and improved performance.

9. To avoid common pitfalls when working with subqueries, remember these best practices:

- **Keep subqueries simple**: Try to limit the complexity of your subqueries. If a subquery is too complex, consider breaking it into smaller parts or using joins or temporary tables instead.

- **Use appropriate operators**: Be mindful of the comparison operators used in subqueries. For example, if you expect a subquery to return a single value, use operators like = or `IN` to handle the results appropriately.

- **Test and optimize**: Always test your subqueries with smaller datasets to ensure they're working as expected. As your data grows, subqueries can become slower, so consider optimizing them through indexing or query rewriting.

10. In conclusion, subqueries and nested queries are essential tools in SQL that allow you to break down complex problems and extract meaningful insights from your data. Whether used in the `WHERE`, `SELECT`, or `FROM` clauses, subqueries give you the flexibility to calculate values, filter data, and perform operations that would otherwise require multiple queries or tables. By mastering subqueries, you can handle complex queries more efficiently and gain deeper insights into your data.

11. In the next chapter, we will take your SQL skills to the next level by exploring **window functions**, which allow you to perform calculations across a set of rows related to the current row. These functions are widely used for running totals, rankings, and other sophisticated analytical tasks. So, get ready to enhance your query-writing skills even further as we dive into the world of window functions! But for now, keep practicing your subqueries, experiment with nested queries, and continue exploring the power of SQL in your data analyses. Happy querying!

12. As we've explored, subqueries offer flexibility in SQL by allowing us to embed one query inside another, enabling complex logic in a single query. However, to fully leverage the power of subqueries, it's important to understand when and why you should use them, as well as how to handle potential performance bottlenecks. Another important aspect is **correlated subqueries**, which are different from regular subqueries because they depend on values from the outer query.

13. A **correlated subquery** is a subquery that refers to a column from the outer query. Unlike a regular subquery, which is independent and can be executed on its own, a correlated subquery needs the context of the outer query to function. Let's say you want to find customers who've placed orders with a total price greater than their average spending. You can use a correlated subquery to compare each customer's total order price with their own average spending:

```
SELECT first_name, last_name FROM customers c WHERE EXISTS
(SELECT 1 FROM orders o WHERE o.customer_id = c.customer_id
AND o.total_price > (SELECT AVG(total_price) FROM orders
WHERE customer_id = c.customer_id));
```

In this query, the subquery references the `customer_id` from the outer query (`c.customer_id`) to calculate the average total price for each individual customer. The subquery is executed for each customer row, making it "correlated." Correlated subqueries are powerful, but they can be performance-heavy because they execute once for each row in the outer query.

14. Another example of a correlated subquery can be used when you want to compare records in one table to the values in the same table. Let's say we have an `employees` table where each employee has a `salary` and a `department_id`, and we want to find employees who earn more than the average salary in their department. Here's how you can write the query:

```
SELECT first_name, last_name, salary FROM employees e WHERE
salary > (SELECT AVG(salary) FROM employees WHERE
```

```
department_id = e.department_id);
```
In this case, the subquery calculates the average salary for each department, and the outer query compares each employee's salary to the average of their department. This makes the subquery "correlated" because it uses the `department_id` from the outer query.

15. While correlated subqueries are powerful, they can be less efficient than joins, especially when they are used with large datasets. This is because the subquery is evaluated for each row of the outer query, which can lead to performance issues. When possible, consider using **joins** instead of correlated subqueries. Joins are typically more efficient because they allow SQL to optimize the query plan by processing both tables together in a single pass, rather than executing a subquery for each row.

16. If performance becomes an issue with correlated subqueries, consider using **temporary tables** or **common table expressions (CTEs)**. These alternatives allow you to store intermediate results from subqueries in memory, which can help optimize complex queries. For example, you could first use a subquery or a CTE to calculate the average salary for each department and then join the result with the `employees` table to get the list of employees earning more than the department's average salary. This approach reduces the number of times the subquery needs to be executed, which can improve performance.

17. One advantage of **Common Table Expressions (CTEs)** over subqueries is their readability. A CTE is essentially a temporary result set that you can reference within your main query. Unlike subqueries, which are typically written inline and can get messy in complex queries, a CTE is defined at the top of your query, making it more readable and easier to debug. You can use CTEs for complex subqueries that you want to reuse multiple times within a query. For example, let's rewrite the previous correlated subquery using a CTE:
```
WITH department_avg_salary AS (SELECT department_id,
AVG(salary) AS avg_salary FROM employees GROUP BY
department_id) SELECT e.first_name, e.last_name, e.salary
FROM employees e INNER JOIN department_avg_salary d ON
e.department_id = d.department_id WHERE e.salary >
d.avg_salary;
```
Here, we use the `WITH` clause to define a CTE that calculates the average salary by department. The main query then joins this CTE with the `employees` table to find employees who earn more than the department average. This approach is not only more readable, but it can also improve performance in some cases.

18. Another key consideration when using subqueries is **nesting depth**. As mentioned earlier, deeply nested subqueries can become complex and harder to maintain. It's a good practice to limit the depth of nested subqueries to avoid excessive complexity. Instead, you should consider breaking down complicated queries into multiple smaller parts, using views or CTEs to hold intermediate results. This will improve both performance and query readability.

19. Subqueries are incredibly useful when you need to perform calculations or filter data based on a condition that can't easily be achieved with a simple join. They allow you to isolate specific logic and retrieve data in stages, making them perfect for multi-step queries. However, it's important to remember that as useful as they are, subqueries should be used judiciously. Always consider whether there's a more efficient alternative, such as using joins, indexing your data properly, or leveraging CTEs.

20. To summarize, subqueries are a versatile tool in SQL that allow you to break down complex problems and perform multi-step data analysis in a single query. Whether used in the `WHERE`, `SELECT`, or `FROM` clauses, subqueries enable you to retrieve and process data in powerful ways. The key is knowing when to use them and being mindful of performance. With nested queries, correlated subqueries, and other advanced techniques, you can handle even the most intricate data tasks.

21. As you continue to work with SQL, keep experimenting with subqueries, particularly nested and correlated ones, and test their performance with your data. The more you use subqueries, the more comfortable and efficient you will become with crafting complex queries. In the next chapter, we'll dive into **window functions**, which allow you to perform calculations across a set of rows related to the current row without collapsing them into a single result. These functions provide additional flexibility in analytical queries, helping you perform running totals, rankings, and other complex operations. So, keep refining your SQL skills, and get ready for the next step in your data journey. Happy querying!

Chapter 9: Data Modification: INSERT, UPDATE, and DELETE

1. Congratulations on making it to the next level of SQL! So far, you've been a master at querying and extracting data, but what happens when you need to change the data inside your tables? Enter **data modification**. Unlike the `SELECT` statement, which retrieves data, the `INSERT`, `UPDATE`, and `DELETE` commands allow you to modify the data stored in your database. Whether you're adding new records, making updates, or removing old entries, mastering these commands is essential for working with databases in real-world applications. In this chapter, we'll break down each of these powerful SQL commands and show you how to safely and efficiently modify data.

2. Let's start with **INSERT**. The `INSERT` statement is used to add new rows to a table. Whether you're adding data one row at a time or inserting multiple rows at once, the syntax is pretty simple. To add a new record into a table, you use `INSERT INTO` followed by the table name and the values you want to insert. For example, suppose you have a `customers` table with columns `customer_id`, `first_name`, `last_name`, and `email`. To add a new customer to the table, you would write:
```
INSERT INTO customers (first_name, last_name, email) VALUES
('John', 'Doe', 'john.doe@example.com');
```
In this example, we specify the column names we want to insert into and then provide the corresponding values. Notice that the `customer_id` column is not included—this could be an auto-incremented primary key, so it's automatically handled by the database.

3. You can also insert multiple rows at once using a single `INSERT` statement, which can save time and effort when adding large sets of data. For example, to insert multiple customers, you could write:

```
INSERT INTO customers (first_name, last_name, email) VALUES
('Jane', 'Smith', 'jane.smith@example.com'), ('Bob',
'Johnson', 'bob.johnson@example.com'), ('Alice',
'Williams', 'alice.williams@example.com');
```

This statement inserts three new records in a single query. Keep in mind that inserting many rows at once is typically more efficient than running multiple individual `INSERT` queries, especially when dealing with large datasets.

4. Next up, we have **UPDATE**. The `UPDATE` statement allows you to modify existing records in a table. This is useful when you need to correct or change data that's already been entered. The `UPDATE` statement has a simple structure: you specify the table to update, the columns to modify, and the new values. For example, if you want to update a customer's email address, you would write:

```
UPDATE customers SET email = 'new.email@example.com' WHERE
customer_id = 1;
```

This query updates the `email` column of the `customers` table, but only for the customer with a `customer_id` of 1. The `WHERE` clause is crucial here—it ensures that only the targeted rows are updated. Without a `WHERE` clause, the query would update all rows in the table, which is a common mistake that can lead to unintended changes to your data.

5. It's important to note that the `UPDATE` statement can modify multiple rows at once if the `WHERE` clause matches multiple records. For instance, if you want to update the email addresses of all customers living in a specific city, you could write:

```
UPDATE customers SET email = 'new.email@example.com' WHERE
city = 'New York';
```

This query will update the `email` for all customers in New York. It's a powerful tool, but be cautious when using broad `WHERE` conditions, as it's easy to accidentally update more data than intended.

6. Now, let's talk about **DELETE**. The `DELETE` statement is used to remove records from a table. This is useful when you need to clean up old or irrelevant data. The `DELETE` statement works similarly to `UPDATE` in that you specify the table and a `WHERE` clause to filter which rows to delete. For example, if you want to delete a customer with a specific `customer_id`, you would write:

```
DELETE FROM customers WHERE customer_id = 1;
```

This query deletes the row where the `customer_id` is 1. Just like with `UPDATE`, the `WHERE` clause is essential for ensuring that only the intended rows are deleted. If you omit the `WHERE` clause, you'll remove **all** rows from the table, which can lead to a complete data loss— something you definitely want to avoid!

7. If you need to delete multiple records at once, you can use a more complex `WHERE` clause to target specific sets of data. For example, if you wanted to delete all customers who have not placed an order in the last year, you might write something like:

```
DELETE FROM customers WHERE last_order_date < '2023-01-01';
```

This query deletes customers whose last order was before January 1, 2023. As always, make sure that your `WHERE` clause is as specific as possible to avoid removing data that you don't intend to delete.

8. It's worth mentioning that `DELETE` is a **permanent operation**. Once data is deleted, it's gone unless you have backups in place or use transaction control statements like **ROLLBACK** to undo the change. For this reason, it's always a good practice to perform a **SELECT** query with the same `WHERE` clause before executing a `DELETE`. For instance:

```
SELECT * FROM customers WHERE customer_id = 1;
```

This lets you preview the data you're about to delete, helping to prevent mistakes.

9. Speaking of safety, SQL also provides a way to safeguard your data modifications with **transactions**. A transaction is a sequence of one or more SQL operations that are executed as a single unit. If any part of the transaction fails, all changes made during the transaction can be rolled back, ensuring that your database remains consistent. Here's a simple example using `BEGIN TRANSACTION`, `COMMIT`, and `ROLLBACK`:

```
BEGIN TRANSACTION; UPDATE customers SET email =
'new.email@example.com' WHERE customer_id = 1; DELETE FROM
customers WHERE customer_id = 2; COMMIT;
```

In this example, the `BEGIN TRANSACTION` starts a new transaction, the `UPDATE` and `DELETE` operations are performed, and `COMMIT` saves the changes. If something goes wrong during the transaction, you can use `ROLLBACK` to undo all changes and keep the database in its original state. Transactions are crucial when you need to ensure that a set of modifications happens together or not at all.

10. In some cases, you may want to **soft delete** records rather than permanently removing them. Soft deleting involves marking records as deleted without actually removing them from the database, allowing for potential recovery later. This is often done by adding a `deleted` flag or a `deleted_at` timestamp column. For example:

```
UPDATE customers SET deleted = 1, deleted_at = NOW() WHERE
customer_id = 1;
```

This marks the customer as deleted but keeps the record in the database for reference or recovery purposes. Soft deletes are useful for systems that need to maintain historical records or perform data recovery.

11. To summarize, the ability to modify data with `INSERT`, `UPDATE`, and `DELETE` is essential for working with SQL databases. Whether you're adding new records, updating existing ones, or removing old data, these commands give you full control over your data. However, it's important to always use caution when modifying data. Always ensure you have the correct `WHERE` conditions to target only the intended rows, and consider using transactions or soft deletes when working with sensitive or critical data.

12. In the next chapter, we will dive into **joins and subqueries** more deeply and explore how they can be combined with `INSERT`, `UPDATE`, and `DELETE` operations to perform advanced data manipulation. These powerful SQL features allow you to combine, update, and delete data from multiple tables at once. So keep practicing these data modification commands, and get ready for the next step in your SQL journey! Happy querying!

13. As you continue to work with data modification commands, it's crucial to understand the importance of **data integrity**. Ensuring that the changes you make to the data do not compromise the quality or consistency of the database is essential. One way to maintain integrity when using `INSERT`, `UPDATE`, or `DELETE` is by implementing **constraints** and **referential integrity**. Constraints such as `NOT NULL`, `UNIQUE`, `PRIMARY KEY`, and `FOREIGN KEY` help enforce rules about the data stored in your tables, ensuring that your modifications do not violate any database rules.

14. For example, when inserting data into a table, make sure that the fields that require a value, such as a `PRIMARY KEY` or `NOT NULL` column, are correctly populated. Inserting `NULL` values into fields that are not allowed to have them can lead to data inconsistency or integrity issues. If you try to insert a record with a `NULL` value into a column defined as `NOT NULL`, the database will raise an error. Similarly, foreign keys ensure that you are inserting valid references to rows in other tables, maintaining relational integrity across your database. It's important to test your `INSERT`, `UPDATE`, and `DELETE` operations against these constraints to avoid violations.

15. Let's explore some best practices to ensure the smooth execution of data modification queries. One of the most crucial practices is to **back up your data** before performing significant `UPDATE` or `DELETE` operations. Especially when working with live production databases, it's important to have a backup in case things go wrong. Even if you're using a transaction to modify data, having a recent backup gives you the peace of mind that you can recover lost or incorrectly modified data.

16. Additionally, using **logging** or **audit tables** can help you track changes to your data over time. For example, you can create an audit table that stores old values whenever an `UPDATE` or `DELETE` operation is performed. This helps you to track changes and even reverse those changes if necessary. Here's how an audit table could look:

```
CREATE TABLE audit_log ( change_id INT PRIMARY KEY
AUTO_INCREMENT, table_name VARCHAR(255), old_value TEXT,
new_value TEXT, change_timestamp TIMESTAMP DEFAULT
CURRENT_TIMESTAMP, action_type VARCHAR(10) );
```

Whenever an `UPDATE` is performed, you would insert the previous values into this audit log, keeping a record of what was changed. This is particularly useful in environments where compliance or data accountability is crucial.

17. When working with **large datasets**, it's also important to be aware of the **impact of data modifications** on performance. Running a `DELETE` operation on a large table, for example, could lock the table for an extended period, preventing other operations from being performed. In these cases, consider **batch processing** your modifications. Instead of deleting or updating all rows in a single operation, break the query into smaller chunks. For example, delete records in batches by specifying a condition that limits the rows affected (such as `DELETE FROM table WHERE id BETWEEN 1 AND 1000;`), and then repeat the operation until all rows are deleted.

18. If you're working with **large data sets** and need to `UPDATE` multiple records efficiently, another approach is to use **bulk updates**. Depending on your database system, you can optimize updates by using **bulk insert** or **bulk update** tools, which can drastically improve performance compared to processing rows individually. For instance, in some systems, you can load data into a temporary table and then use a join to update the main table in one operation, making it faster and more efficient.

19. Another important consideration is the **locking behavior** during data modification operations. When you `INSERT`, `UPDATE`, or `DELETE` data, your SQL database may lock the affected rows or even entire tables to prevent data inconsistency caused by concurrent transactions. Different databases handle locking in different ways, but be aware that if you have multiple users or applications working on the same database, modifying data could result in lock contention, leading to performance bottlenecks. In cases where this becomes an issue, consider using **transaction isolation levels** to control how your transactions interact with each other. By adjusting the isolation level, you can control whether your changes are immediately visible to other users or if the changes will be blocked until the transaction is committed.

20. It's also worth noting that **cascading actions** are a feature of the `FOREIGN KEY` constraint, which can be incredibly useful for keeping related tables in sync. For example, when you delete a customer record from the `customers` table, you may want to automatically delete all their orders from the `orders` table. This is where **cascade delete** comes in. When defining a `FOREIGN KEY` relationship, you can specify that deletions or updates on the primary table should cascade to the related table. Here's an example of how to create a cascading delete:
`ALTER TABLE orders ADD CONSTRAINT fk_customer_id FOREIGN KEY (customer_id) REFERENCES customers(customer_id) ON DELETE CASCADE;`
With this setting, deleting a record from the `customers` table will automatically remove all related records from the `orders` table, ensuring that your database remains consistent without requiring additional `DELETE` operations.

21. As we near the end of this chapter, it's clear that data modification is a critical skill for any SQL user. By mastering `INSERT`, `UPDATE`, and `DELETE`, you'll be able to effectively manage and modify the data in your database, whether you're adding new records, updating existing ones, or removing outdated data. Always keep in mind best practices, such as using transactions, being cautious with WHERE clauses, and backing up data before performing any destructive operations.

22. In the next chapter, we'll look into **stored procedures** and **triggers**, which allow you to automate and encapsulate complex operations in SQL. These features are great for ensuring consistency and streamlining your workflows, especially when you need to perform repetitive tasks or automatically respond to certain changes in your data. So, continue experimenting with your data modification skills, and get ready to dive into the world of stored procedures and triggers. Happy querying and modifying!

Chapter 10: Working with Constraints and Indexes

1. Welcome to one of the most important chapters in SQL—**constraints** and **indexes**. As you continue to work with databases, it becomes crucial to maintain the integrity, consistency, and efficiency of the data stored within them. That's where constraints and indexes come in. Constraints allow you to define rules and restrictions on your data, ensuring that it remains clean and consistent. Indexes, on the other hand, help improve query performance by allowing the database to quickly locate and retrieve data. In this chapter, we'll explore both concepts in depth and show you how they play a vital role in database design and optimization.

2. Let's start with **constraints**. A constraint is a rule applied to a column or table to ensure the accuracy and integrity of the data in the database. Constraints are important because they help ensure that data is entered correctly and adheres to certain rules. There are several types of constraints, including NOT NULL, UNIQUE, PRIMARY KEY, FOREIGN KEY, and CHECK. Each type of constraint serves a different purpose, and understanding how to use them properly will help you design more reliable and secure databases.

3. The **NOT NULL** constraint ensures that a column cannot have a NULL value. This is essential when you want to make sure that certain fields always contain data. For example, in a customers table, it's unlikely that a customer should have an empty email address, so you would apply the NOT NULL constraint to the email column:

```
CREATE TABLE customers ( customer_id INT PRIMARY KEY,
first_name VARCHAR(50), last_name VARCHAR(50), email
VARCHAR(100) NOT NULL );
```

With this constraint in place, any attempt to insert a NULL value into the email column will result in an error. Using NOT NULL ensures that essential information is always provided.

4. The **UNIQUE** constraint is used to ensure that all values in a column are different. This is useful for fields like email addresses or username, where each value must be unique across the table. Here's an example of how to use the UNIQUE constraint:

```
CREATE TABLE users ( user_id INT PRIMARY KEY, username
VARCHAR(50) UNIQUE, email VARCHAR(100) UNIQUE );
```

In this case, both username and email columns have the UNIQUE constraint, meaning no two users can have the same username or email address. This is crucial for systems that require uniqueness, like social media platforms or online stores.

5. The **PRIMARY KEY** constraint is a combination of both the NOT NULL and UNIQUE constraints. It uniquely identifies each row in a table and ensures that the column or set of columns defined as the primary key has no NULL values and contains only unique values. In most cases, the primary key is used for a column like ID that uniquely identifies each record in the table:

```
CREATE TABLE employees ( employee_id INT PRIMARY KEY,
first_name VARCHAR(50), last_name VARCHAR(50) );
```

In this case, employee_id is the primary key. Every row must have a unique, non-NULL value in this column, which allows you to uniquely identify each employee.

6. While indexes are incredibly powerful tools for improving query performance, it's essential to consider the **maintenance cost** that comes with them. As I mentioned earlier, while indexes speed up data retrieval, they can slow down **data modification operations** such as INSERT, UPDATE, and DELETE. This happens because every time a row is added, updated, or deleted, the associated indexes must be updated as well. For example, if you have a composite index on three columns in a table, every time a row is inserted or updated, the database must update all three columns in the index. In environments with high transaction volumes, this additional overhead can become significant, so it's critical to carefully plan which columns to index based on the types of queries you will be running most often.

7. Another performance consideration with indexes is the **type of index** you use. While the default index type for most databases is a **B-tree index**, there are other types of indexes that may be more appropriate for certain use cases. For example, **hash indexes** are useful for equality searches, where you need to match a specific value exactly, such as in WHERE column = value. Hash indexes are typically faster than B-tree indexes for these exact match lookups, but they don't support range queries (e.g., BETWEEN or > <), so they are not suitable for all situations. Similarly, **full-text indexes** are specialized for searching text-based data and are particularly useful in applications that require searching large text fields like blog posts or product descriptions.

8. In addition to **primary indexes** and **unique indexes**, you can also create **partial indexes**. A **partial index** is an index built on a subset of the rows in a table, based on a specific condition. This can be especially useful if you only need to optimize performance for a certain subset of your data. For example, if you only frequently query active customers, you can create a partial index on the customers table where the status column is set to "active":

```
CREATE INDEX idx_active_customers ON customers (last_name)
WHERE status = 'active';
```

This index would only include rows where the status is "active," thus reducing storage and improving query performance for queries that focus on active customers. It's a great way to fine-tune your indexing strategy for performance-sensitive applications.

9. Now that we've covered some of the intricacies of indexes, let's circle back to **constraints** and explore their role in **enforcing business rules**. In addition to the standard constraints like `PRIMARY KEY`, `FOREIGN KEY`, and `CHECK`, you can also use **trigger-based constraints** to implement rules that are more complex and cannot easily be expressed through traditional constraints. For example, you might want to enforce a rule that prevents the deletion of any customer who has associated orders. While a `FOREIGN KEY` constraint with `ON DELETE RESTRICT` can prevent this action, triggers allow you to define even more complex behaviors.

10. A **trigger** is a special type of stored procedure that is automatically executed (or "triggered") when a certain event occurs on a table. This event can be an `INSERT`, `UPDATE`, or `DELETE` operation. Triggers are useful for enforcing constraints and automating actions in response to specific database changes. For example, if you want to make sure that when a customer is deleted, any associated orders are archived instead of just being deleted, you could create a trigger to automatically copy the order data into an archive table before the delete operation is performed. Here's an example of a basic delete trigger in SQL:

```
CREATE TRIGGER archive_customer_orders BEFORE DELETE ON
customers FOR EACH ROW BEGIN INSERT INTO archived_orders
SELECT * FROM orders WHERE customer_id = OLD.customer_id;
END;
```

In this example, before a customer is deleted, the trigger automatically copies their orders to the `archived_orders` table, ensuring no data is lost during the deletion process.

11. When working with triggers, it's essential to be mindful of performance. Since triggers automatically execute whenever the associated event occurs, they can add overhead to data modification operations. For example, if a trigger performs an `INSERT` into another table or performs complex calculations, it may slow down your queries. Because triggers are executed as part of the transaction, if the trigger encounters an error, it will cause the entire transaction to roll back, which is something to consider when writing them. It's always a good idea to keep triggers as efficient as possible, especially when working in high-traffic databases.

12. Indexes and **constraints** are key elements in designing an efficient and consistent database, but remember, they are not silver bullets. While they help maintain data integrity and performance, improper use of indexes or constraints can lead to unexpected behavior or inefficiencies. For example, over-indexing (creating too many indexes) can significantly slow down `INSERT`, `UPDATE`, and `DELETE` operations because of the added overhead of maintaining the indexes. Similarly, using `CHECK` constraints for overly complex rules can impact performance, especially when dealing with large datasets. Always consider trade-offs carefully and test your database schema to make sure it meets your performance requirements.

13. In some cases, you might find that you need to **drop or disable** an index temporarily for performance reasons. SQL allows you to do this with the `DROP INDEX` or `ALTER INDEX` commands, depending on your database system. For example, you might disable an index while performing large bulk inserts and then re-enable it afterward to optimize query performance. This is particularly useful for large data import or migration tasks where indexes can slow down the process. Here's an example of how to drop and recreate an index:

```
DROP INDEX idx_last_name;
CREATE INDEX idx_last_name ON customers (last_name);
```
Remember to re-create the index after data modifications are completed to ensure your queries remain optimized.

14. Finally, it's important to note that some databases support **indexing on views**. A view is essentially a virtual table that contains the result of a query. While views themselves don't store data, they can be indexed in some databases to optimize performance when the view is queried repeatedly. Indexing views can be particularly helpful when working with complex queries or aggregations that you frequently run, as it allows the database to avoid recalculating the result each time.

15. In conclusion, both constraints and indexes are critical components of a well-designed SQL database. Constraints help enforce the integrity and consistency of your data, while indexes dramatically improve query performance by allowing the database to quickly locate and retrieve the necessary rows. However, you should always carefully consider the performance implications of both, as overuse can lead to inefficiencies. Striking the right balance is key to creating an optimized and reliable database that supports the needs of your application.

16. In the next chapter, we will explore **stored procedures** and **triggers** in more detail, giving you the tools to automate tasks and encapsulate complex logic in your database. These features are ideal for improving efficiency, maintaining business logic, and managing repetitive tasks. So, keep practicing with constraints and indexes, and get ready to dive into the automation capabilities of SQL in the next chapter. Happy querying!

17. As we continue our exploration of **indexes**, it's important to understand the concept of **index maintenance**. As your database grows and evolves over time, the effectiveness of indexes can decrease due to factors like data fragmentation, changes in query patterns, and increased data volume. Regular maintenance, such as **index rebuilding** or **index reorganization**, can help ensure that your indexes remain efficient. For example, in databases like SQL Server or PostgreSQL, you can rebuild indexes to eliminate fragmentation and restore their performance. Here's an example of rebuilding an index in SQL Server:
```
ALTER INDEX idx_last_name ON customers REBUILD;
```
This command rebuilds the `idx_last_name` index on the `customers` table, optimizing its structure and ensuring faster query performance. Depending on the database system you use, tools for index maintenance may vary, but it's important to monitor index performance over time and rebuild or reorganize them as needed.

18. It's also worth mentioning that **composite indexes**—indexes built on multiple columns—can sometimes improve performance for queries that filter or sort by several columns simultaneously. For example, suppose you frequently query your `orders` table by both `customer_id` and `order_date`. Instead of creating separate indexes on `customer_id` and `order_date`, you can create a composite index that includes both columns:
```
CREATE INDEX idx_customer_order_date ON orders
(customer_id, order_date);
```

This composite index helps the database more efficiently retrieve data based on both columns. However, as with all indexes, be sure to evaluate your query patterns to determine if composite indexes are necessary. Over-indexing, especially on multiple-column indexes, can lead to slower performance on data modification operations.

19. Another important index-related topic is **covering indexes**. A covering index is an index that contains all the columns needed by a query, so the database can fulfill the query entirely from the index without having to look at the actual table data. This can drastically speed up query performance, as accessing the index is much faster than reading from the table itself. For example, if you frequently run a query like this:

```
SELECT customer_id, order_date, total_price FROM orders
WHERE customer_id = 123;
```

You could create a covering index on `customer_id`, `order_date`, and `total_price` like this:

```
CREATE INDEX idx_customer_orders_cover ON orders
(customer_id, order_date, total_price);
```

This index covers all the columns required by the query, meaning the database can retrieve the necessary information directly from the index without accessing the underlying table. Covering indexes are particularly useful for read-heavy applications where the same queries are executed frequently.

20. Moving on from indexes, let's talk about **constraint naming conventions**. When creating constraints, especially in larger databases with many tables, it's essential to follow a consistent naming convention. This ensures that your database schema remains readable and maintainable. A good naming convention might include the table name, the type of constraint, and the columns involved. For example, for a foreign key on the `customer_id` column in the `orders` table, a good name might be:

```
fk_orders_customer_id
```

Similarly, a check constraint that ensures an order's total price is greater than zero could be named:

```
chk_orders_total_price
```

By following clear naming conventions, you make it easier for others (or even yourself) to understand and maintain the database schema in the future.

21. Another important aspect of **constraints** is **enforcing business rules**. Some business rules can't be easily enforced through basic constraints like NOT NULL or CHECK. In these cases, you can use **triggers** or **stored procedures** to ensure that your data adheres to specific rules. For instance, let's say you have a rule that no customer should have an order total greater than their available credit. While you can't enforce this with a simple CHECK constraint, you can use a trigger to prevent the insertion of such an order:

```
CREATE TRIGGER check_order_credit BEFORE INSERT ON orders
FOR EACH ROW BEGIN IF NEW.total_price > (SELECT
credit_limit FROM customers WHERE customer_id =
NEW.customer_id) THEN SIGNAL SQLSTATE '45000' SET
```

```
MESSAGE_TEXT = 'Order total exceeds available credit'; END
IF; END;
```
This trigger prevents any order with a total price greater than the available credit limit from being inserted into the `orders` table. Triggers provide flexibility in enforcing complex business rules that go beyond the capabilities of standard constraints.

22. While triggers are powerful, they should be used carefully, especially in high-traffic databases. Since triggers execute automatically, they can sometimes lead to unexpected delays or resource consumption. It's important to ensure that your triggers are as efficient as possible. For example, avoid making complex calculations or performing multiple queries within a trigger, as this can add significant overhead. Always test your triggers thoroughly to ensure they don't negatively impact performance, especially when the trigger logic is tied to high-volume operations like `INSERT`, `UPDATE`, or `DELETE`.

23. Another important concept is **cascading actions**. Cascading actions are a feature of the `FOREIGN KEY` constraint that automatically perform actions on related rows when the parent row is updated or deleted. These actions can be defined as `ON DELETE CASCADE`, `ON UPDATE CASCADE`, or `ON DELETE SET NULL`, depending on how you want the system to behave when a change occurs. Let's consider a scenario where you have two tables: `customers` and `orders`, and you want to automatically delete all orders related to a customer when that customer is deleted. Here's how you could define this using cascading actions:
```
ALTER TABLE orders ADD CONSTRAINT fk_customer_id FOREIGN
KEY (customer_id) REFERENCES customers(customer_id) ON
DELETE CASCADE;
```
With this constraint, when a customer is deleted from the `customers` table, all associated orders will automatically be deleted from the `orders` table, ensuring referential integrity without requiring any additional operations.

24. In conclusion, **constraints** and **indexes** are foundational tools in SQL that help maintain the integrity and performance of your database. Constraints ensure that your data remains accurate, consistent, and adheres to business rules, while indexes provide efficient data retrieval for faster query performance. Both of these features are essential when working with large, dynamic databases. Understanding how to properly use and maintain constraints and indexes will ensure that your SQL database performs well and remains reliable as it grows.

25. In the next chapter, we'll dive into **stored procedures** and **triggers** in more detail, showing you how to automate tasks and encapsulate business logic in your database. These features are especially useful for managing complex operations and ensuring consistency across your database. By the end of that chapter, you'll be able to take your SQL skills to the next level by writing custom procedures and triggers that simplify your workflows. So, keep practicing with constraints and indexes, and get ready to automate your SQL world! Happy querying and optimizing!

Chapter 11: Data Normalization and Database Design

1. Welcome to one of the most important chapters in SQL—**data normalization** and **database design**! At this stage in your SQL journey, you're learning how to query and manipulate data efficiently, but it's equally important to understand how to structure your database in a way that maximizes performance, consistency, and flexibility. Proper database design is key to ensuring that your data is stored efficiently, is easy to maintain, and prevents unnecessary duplication. In this chapter, we'll dive into the concept of **data normalization**, a process that helps eliminate redundancy and improves data integrity. We'll also explore best practices in database design that will help you build scalable, reliable databases that are easy to work with.

2. Let's start by defining **data normalization**. Normalization is the process of organizing the attributes (columns) and tables of a relational database to minimize redundancy and dependency. The goal is to ensure that the database is free from unnecessary data duplication and that the relationships between tables are logical and easy to maintain. Normalization is achieved by breaking down large tables into smaller, related tables and ensuring that each table stores only the data that pertains to it. While normalization is important, it's essential to balance it with performance needs, as overly normalized databases can sometimes lead to complex queries that perform poorly.

3. First Normal Form (1NF) is the foundation of the normalization process. A table is in 1NF if it satisfies the following conditions:

- All columns contain atomic (indivisible) values.

- Each column contains values of a single type (e.g., all values in a column are integers, strings, etc.).

- Each record in the table must be unique (no duplicate rows).

For example, consider a `students` table where each student can have multiple phone numbers listed in a single column. This table would not be in 1NF because the `phone_numbers` column contains multiple values. To bring the table into 1NF, we would split the phone numbers into separate rows, like so:

student_id	first_name	last_name	phone_number
1	John	Doe	123-456-7890
1	John	Doe	987-654-3210
2	Jane	Smith	555-123-4567

Now, each column contains atomic values, and the table is in 1NF.

4. Second Normal Form (2NF) builds on 1NF by eliminating partial dependencies. A table is in 2NF if it satisfies two conditions:

1. It must first be in 1NF.

2. It must not have any partial dependencies, meaning no non-key column is dependent on only a part of a composite primary key.

To understand this, let's look at an example. Suppose you have a `course_enrollments` table that contains the following columns:

- `student_id` (part of the primary key)

- `course_id` (part of the primary key)

- `student_name`

- `course_name`

In this case, `student_name` depends on `student_id`, and `course_name` depends on `course_id`. These are partial dependencies because they don't depend on the full composite key (`student_id` + `course_id`). To move the table into 2NF, you would split it into two tables:

Students Table:

student_id	student_name
1	John Doe
2	Jane Smith

Courses Table:

course_id	course_name
101	Math 101
102	English 101

Now, the `student_name` and `course_name` columns are no longer partially dependent on the composite key, so the tables are in 2NF.

5. Third Normal Form (3NF) goes one step further by eliminating **transitive dependencies**, where one non-key column depends on another non-key column. A table is in 3NF if it satisfies two conditions:

1. It must first be in 2NF.

2. It must not have any transitive dependencies.

Consider a `students` table that includes `student_id`, `student_name`, and `advisor_name`. If `advisor_name` depends on `student_id` indirectly through another column, such as `advisor_id`, this is a transitive dependency. To bring this table into 3NF, you would split it into two tables:

Students Table:

student_id	student_name	advisor_id
1	John Doe	1001
2	Jane Smith	1002

Advisors Table:

advisor_id	advisor_name
1001	Dr. Brown
1002	Dr. Green

Now, there are no transitive dependencies, and the tables are in 3NF.

6. The process of **normalization** continues with **Boyce-Codd Normal Form (BCNF)** and **Fourth Normal Form (4NF)**, but 3NF is typically sufficient for most applications. BCNF deals with situations where a table has multiple candidate keys, and 4NF addresses multi-valued dependencies, but these are advanced topics that are not always necessary in everyday database design. The goal is to normalize your data to a level that minimizes redundancy and complexity while maintaining performance.

7. While normalization is crucial for preventing data redundancy and ensuring data integrity, it's important to note that **over-normalization** can lead to **performance issues**. Highly normalized databases require more joins in queries, which can slow down query performance, especially when working with large datasets. In practice, many developers strike a balance between normalization and performance by applying normalization up to 3NF and then selectively denormalizing certain parts of the database where performance is a concern.

8. Denormalization is the process of intentionally introducing redundancy into a database to improve query performance. This might involve combining tables or adding redundant columns to reduce the need for multiple joins. For example, if you frequently query data from both the `customers` and `orders` tables, and you're willing to sacrifice some storage space, you might denormalize your schema by adding frequently accessed columns (like `customer_name`) directly into the `orders` table. This approach can improve performance, but it also increases the potential for data inconsistency and requires more maintenance.

9. When designing a database, it's important to think about the **relationships** between entities. **Entity-relationship diagrams (ERD)** are commonly used to visually represent the database schema and the relationships between tables. In an ERD, tables are represented as entities, and the relationships between them are shown as lines connecting the entities. The key types of relationships are:

- **One-to-one**: Each row in Table A is related to one row in Table B.

- **One-to-many**: Each row in Table A can be related to multiple rows in Table B.

- **Many-to-many**: Multiple rows in Table A can be related to multiple rows in Table B.

10. When designing your database schema, make sure to normalize your tables to at least 3NF for efficient storage and to eliminate redundancy. However, always keep an eye on performance. **Indexes** can help improve query performance for frequently accessed columns, while **denormalization** should be considered if performance issues arise from heavy joins. Designing a database is an iterative process that requires balancing data integrity with the need for efficient querying.

11. In conclusion, **data normalization** and **database design** are the foundation of an efficient, maintainable, and reliable database. Normalization ensures that data is stored without redundancy, while proper database design ensures that relationships are logical and that data can be accessed efficiently. By applying the principles of normalization and carefully considering performance implications, you'll be well on your way to designing effective databases. As you advance, always consider the specific needs of your application, and be prepared to adjust your design to fit the use case at hand.

12. In the next chapter, we will explore **stored procedures**, which allow you to encapsulate logic and automate tasks within your database. These can simplify complex operations and improve the performance of repeated tasks. So, keep practicing your database design skills, and get ready to dive into the world of stored procedures and advanced SQL techniques. Happy designing and normalizing!

13. Another key aspect of **database design** that ties into normalization is the concept of **referential integrity**. Referential integrity ensures that relationships between tables remain consistent. This means that foreign keys must always point to valid rows in the referenced table, and foreign key constraints enforce this rule. For example, in our `orders` and `customers` tables, the `customer_id` in the `orders` table must correspond to an existing `customer_id` in the `customers` table. If a foreign key constraint is set with `ON DELETE CASCADE`, for instance, deleting a customer will automatically delete all related orders, ensuring that no "orphaned" orders remain.
However, referential integrity can sometimes conflict with performance needs, especially in large systems with frequent updates and deletes. For this reason, carefully consider the implications of cascading actions and how they will affect your system's performance, especially with large data volumes.

14. While **referential integrity** ensures that your database relationships are logically sound, **logical design** also extends to how you **optimize for queries**. Sometimes, the **structure of your**

data must be designed in a way that not only adheres to normalization principles but also takes into account the most common query patterns. If certain queries are run frequently and require data from multiple normalized tables, you may want to **denormalize** those parts of the database to speed up query performance. This often involves adding redundant data in places that would otherwise require multiple joins. However, be cautious with this approach, as denormalization can increase the likelihood of data anomalies and make the system more challenging to maintain.

15. Another important concept related to database design is the **use of surrogate keys**. A surrogate key is an artificial, usually auto-incrementing, identifier that is used as the primary key in a table. Surrogate keys are often preferred over natural keys (which are based on real-world data) because they are simple, unique, and immutable. For example, in a `customers` table, using a `customer_id` as a surrogate key (auto-incremented) is often a better choice than using a natural key like `email_address` or `phone_number`. Surrogate keys provide simplicity and consistency, especially when dealing with large datasets where natural keys may be cumbersome or change over time.

16. Indexes and **normalization** go hand-in-hand when considering database performance. While normalization reduces redundancy and ensures data integrity, it can sometimes lead to performance issues due to the increased number of joins between tables. This is where **indexes** come in. Proper indexing on columns that are frequently used for filtering, sorting, and joining can significantly speed up query performance. However, creating indexes on too many columns or using them on columns that aren't frequently queried can hurt performance by consuming storage space and slowing down insertions, updates, and deletions.

For example, consider a `sales` table where you frequently search by `sale_date`, `product_id`, and `customer_id`. You could create indexes on these columns to speed up retrieval. However, if you add indexes to every column in every table, the overhead of maintaining those indexes can result in slower performance overall. Therefore, index only the columns that will provide the most performance benefit.

17. Database normalization is essential, but you should be aware that in certain situations, **denormalization** is often used in **data warehousing** and **OLAP (Online Analytical Processing)** systems. These systems typically require very fast querying of large amounts of data and can afford to have redundant data to optimize for faster query performance. For instance, **fact tables** in data warehouses often store pre-aggregated data, meaning the data is intentionally duplicated to avoid real-time calculations during query execution. While data redundancy is reduced in OLTP systems (which aim for quick transaction processing), in OLAP systems, **performance is prioritized over redundancy**, making denormalization a useful tool for improving query performance.

18. The decision to normalize or denormalize your database schema depends largely on the **nature of your application**. If you're building an **OLTP (Online Transaction Processing)** system where the focus is on inserting, updating, and deleting transactional data, normalization will help ensure data integrity and consistency, which is crucial for maintaining a high level of reliability. However, if you're building a **data warehouse** or **OLAP system**, where the goal is to perform complex analytical queries on large datasets, denormalization might be the right choice for optimizing performance. Balancing these two approaches depending on your specific use case is essential for creating an optimal database design.

19. Another important consideration in **database design** is ensuring that the design is **scalable**. As the data grows, the database should remain efficient, and its performance should not degrade. One way to ensure scalability is by following the **principles of horizontal scaling**, such as **sharding**. Sharding involves splitting large databases into smaller, more manageable pieces, called shards, and distributing them across multiple servers. This is especially useful for applications with massive datasets, as it ensures that no single server becomes a bottleneck.

20. Vertical scaling — increasing the resources of a single server, such as adding more CPU, memory, or storage — is another method of scaling. However, vertical scaling has its limits, and horizontal scaling (like sharding) becomes the go-to method for truly massive datasets. When designing your database, always consider future growth and potential performance bottlenecks, and plan your data storage, indexing, and partitioning strategies accordingly.

21. Finally, one often overlooked but crucial aspect of **database design** is **security**. As you design your database, it's important to think about who can access your data and what kind of data access is required. Database security involves restricting access to sensitive data through the use of **roles**, **permissions**, and **user authentication**. For example, you may want to give a user access to only a specific subset of the data, such as allowing them to read from one table but not modify it. Additionally, encrypting sensitive data, especially in compliance-heavy industries, helps prevent unauthorized access to your most critical data.

22. In conclusion, **database design** and **data normalization** are fundamental to building efficient, reliable, and scalable databases. By following normalization principles, you ensure that your data remains consistent, and by applying best practices in database design, you ensure that your database is optimized for performance and scalability. Remember, designing a good database is an iterative process. You'll need to continuously refine your design as your application grows and your needs evolve. Understanding the balance between normalization and denormalization, indexes, scalability, and security is key to building a database that works well both today and in the future.

23. In the next chapter, we will dive into **stored procedures** and **triggers**, which will allow you to automate complex operations and encapsulate business logic within the database. These tools will give you the ability to perform tasks more efficiently, automate repetitive tasks, and encapsulate complex SQL queries for reuse. So, keep practicing your database design skills, and get ready to unlock new levels of automation and efficiency in your SQL work. Happy designing!

Chapter 12: Advanced Query Techniques: CASE Statements and CTEs

1. Welcome to one of the most exciting chapters in SQL! In this chapter, we will dive into **advanced query techniques** that will allow you to write more flexible and powerful queries. Specifically, we will cover **CASE statements** and **Common Table Expressions (CTEs)** — two tools that will enhance your ability to manipulate and transform your data. Whether you're adding conditional logic to your queries with CASE or structuring your queries more clearly with CTEs, these techniques will help you tackle complex data manipulation tasks with ease.

2. Let's begin with **CASE statements**. A CASE statement allows you to introduce **conditional logic** directly into your queries. This makes it possible to perform **IF-THEN-ELSE** type logic within your SELECT, UPDATE, and ORDER BY clauses. The CASE statement is like a formula that helps SQL decide which value to return based on a given condition. It's extremely useful for performing transformations, calculations, or even generating new data points based on existing data.

3. There are two main types of CASE statements: **simple CASE** and **searched CASE**. The **simple CASE** statement compares an expression to a series of possible values and returns a result when it finds a match. For example, let's say you want to categorize customers into "VIP," "Regular," and "New" based on their number of orders. Here's how you can write the query:

```
SELECT customer_id, CASE order_count WHEN 0 THEN 'New' WHEN
1 THEN 'Regular' ELSE 'VIP' END AS customer_status FROM
customers;
```

In this case, the CASE statement checks the value of order_count and assigns the appropriate customer status. The WHEN clause checks for specific values, and the ELSE clause provides the default value if no match is found.

4. The **searched CASE** statement is more flexible. It allows you to define a series of conditions that are evaluated in sequence, much like an IF-ELSE IF structure in programming. Let's say you want to categorize orders based on the total price. Here's how you might write it using a searched CASE statement:

```
SELECT order_id, total_price, CASE WHEN total_price < 50
THEN 'Low' WHEN total_price BETWEEN 50 AND 200 THEN
'Medium' ELSE 'High' END AS order_value_category FROM
orders;
```

In this example, the CASE statement evaluates the total_price and assigns an order to one of three categories—'Low,' 'Medium,' or 'High.' The conditionals are evaluated in order until a match is found.

5. One powerful use case for the CASE statement is in generating **dynamic reports** or **calculated fields**. For example, if you want to calculate a **discount** based on the order amount, you can use CASE to assign different discount percentages. Here's an example of how to implement that:

```
SELECT order_id, total_price, CASE WHEN total_price >= 100
THEN total_price * 0.1 WHEN total_price >= 50 THEN
total_price * 0.05 ELSE 0 END AS discount FROM orders;
```

This query calculates the discount based on the total order price, with higher total prices receiving a greater discount. Using CASE like this adds conditional logic directly into the calculation process without needing to modify the underlying data.

6. Another use case for the `CASE` statement is in the **ORDER BY** clause. You can dynamically sort results based on conditions. For example, suppose you have a table of products, and you want to sort them by price but with some special business logic—such as placing out-of-stock products at the bottom of the list. You could write:

```
SELECT product_id, product_name, price, stock_quantity FROM
products ORDER BY CASE WHEN stock_quantity = 0 THEN 1 ELSE
0 END, price DESC;
```

This query first orders the products by stock availability (with out-of-stock items appearing last), and then sorts the remaining items by price in descending order. The flexibility of `CASE` in the `ORDER BY` clause allows you to prioritize data in ways that traditional sorting can't.

7. Now let's move on to **Common Table Expressions (CTEs)**. CTEs are a powerful tool that allows you to define temporary result sets that you can reference multiple times within a query. They can be particularly useful for **complex queries** involving multiple subqueries or joins. CTEs make your queries more **readable** and **modular**, as you can break down your logic into easily understandable pieces.

8. To define a CTE, you use the `WITH` keyword, followed by the name of the CTE and the query that defines it. The CTE can then be referenced in the main query as if it were a regular table. Let's look at an example where we use a CTE to find the total sales for each product before joining it with the `products` table to retrieve the product details:

```
WITH product_sales AS ( SELECT product_id, SUM(total_price)
AS total_sales FROM orders GROUP BY product_id ) SELECT
p.product_id, p.product_name, ps.total_sales FROM products
p JOIN product_sales ps ON p.product_id = ps.product_id;
```

In this example, the CTE `product_sales` calculates the total sales for each product, and the main query joins it with the `products` table to display the product name and total sales. By using a CTE, the query becomes more modular and easier to understand than if we had written everything in a single, complex query.

9. CTEs can also be **recursive**, which means they can refer to themselves. Recursive CTEs are especially useful for working with hierarchical data, such as organizational charts or directory structures. Let's say you have an `employees` table where each employee has a `manager_id`, and you want to retrieve a list of employees along with their direct and indirect reports. You can write a recursive CTE like this:

```
WITH RECURSIVE employee_hierarchy AS ( SELECT employee_id,
first_name, last_name, manager_id FROM employees WHERE
manager_id IS NULL UNION ALL SELECT e.employee_id,
e.first_name, e.last_name, e.manager_id FROM employees e
INNER JOIN employee_hierarchy eh ON e.manager_id =
eh.employee_id ) SELECT * FROM employee_hierarchy;
```

In this example, the recursive CTE `employee_hierarchy` starts with employees who don't have a manager (i.e., the top-level employees) and then recursively adds their reports by joining with the CTE. The `UNION ALL` combines the base case (employees without managers) with the recursive case (employees managed by someone already in the hierarchy).

10. CTEs also allow you to **reuse** the same temporary result set in multiple places within a query. This makes them an excellent choice when you need to refer to the same intermediate result in multiple parts of your query. This avoids writing the same subquery multiple times and improves query readability. For example, you might use a CTE to calculate sales totals for different regions and then use the results in multiple parts of your query to perform further analysis.

11. The combination of **CASE statements** and **CTEs** is particularly powerful when you're working with complex data transformations. For example, if you need to calculate discounts based on certain conditions (using `CASE`) and then aggregate sales by region using a CTE, you can combine both techniques to build a clean, efficient query. This modular approach is incredibly useful for building queries that are easy to understand, maintain, and optimize.

12. In conclusion, **CASE statements** and **CTEs** are two advanced techniques that allow you to write flexible, powerful SQL queries. The `CASE` statement enables you to introduce conditional logic directly into your queries, making it easier to perform transformations, calculations, and categorizations based on specific conditions. **CTEs**, on the other hand, help you structure complex queries in a more readable and modular way, and recursive CTEs are an excellent tool for working with hierarchical data. Together, these techniques allow you to handle some of the most complex and dynamic queries in SQL.

13. In the next chapter, we'll dive into **advanced SQL functions**, such as **window functions**, that allow you to perform calculations across a set of rows related to the current row without collapsing them into a single result. These functions are essential for running totals, rankings, and moving averages, which are often used in reporting and data analysis. Get ready for more powerful SQL techniques to add to your arsenal! Happy querying!

Chapter 12: Advanced Query Techniques: CASE Statements and CTEs (Continued)

14. As we continue discussing **CTEs** and **CASE statements**, it's worth mentioning that **CTEs** can improve the **reusability** and **readability** of your SQL code. When you have complex queries with multiple joins, subqueries, or calculations, breaking them into separate, understandable pieces using CTEs can make your query much easier to follow and debug. This is especially beneficial in large projects where multiple developers work on the same database. A good practice is to define CTEs for each individual task or logical part of the query. For instance, if you are calculating total sales, filtering by region, and categorizing customers into segments, you could break these tasks into separate CTEs, as shown below:

```sql
Copy
WITH total_sales AS (
   SELECT customer_id, SUM(total_price) AS sales
   FROM orders
   GROUP BY customer_id
```

```sql
),
region_sales AS (
   SELECT customer_id, region
   FROM customers
   WHERE region IS NOT NULL
),
customer_segments AS (
   SELECT customer_id,
         CASE
            WHEN sales >= 1000 THEN 'High'
            WHEN sales >= 500 THEN 'Medium'
            ELSE 'Low'
         END AS customer_segment
   FROM total_sales
)
SELECT cs.customer_id, cs.customer_segment, rs.region
FROM customer_segments cs
JOIN region_sales rs ON cs.customer_id = rs.customer_id;
```
In this example, each logical step (calculating total sales, categorizing customers, filtering by region) is handled by a separate CTE. This modular approach makes the query easier to read and debug, allowing you to focus on each part of the logic individually.

15. Another advanced feature of **CTEs** is the ability to **chain multiple CTEs together**. You can use one CTE as a foundation for another, creating a clear flow of logic. For example, let's say you need to calculate the average order value per customer, then calculate how many customers have orders above this average. You could chain CTEs together like this:

```sql
sql
Copy
WITH avg_order_value AS (
   SELECT customer_id, AVG(total_price) AS avg_price
   FROM orders
   GROUP BY customer_id
),
high_value_customers AS (
   SELECT o.customer_id
   FROM orders o
   JOIN avg_order_value aov ON o.customer_id =
aov.customer_id
   WHERE o.total_price > aov.avg_price
)
SELECT COUNT(*) AS high_value_count
```

```
FROM high_value_customers;
```
In this query, the first CTE calculates the average order value per customer, and the second CTE identifies customers whose order total exceeds that average. By chaining these CTEs, the logic is clearly divided into two stages, and you can use the result of one CTE in another.

16. While **CASE statements** and **CTEs** are incredibly powerful tools in SQL, it's important to understand when and how to **combine** them effectively for maximum performance and readability. One powerful use case is when you need to apply multiple conditions and transformations to your data, and you want to break down the logic into distinct, manageable parts. For example, you may want to categorize data based on several complex conditions, then aggregate or rank the data based on these categories. Combining **CASE** statements with **CTEs** allows you to keep the logic modular, reducing the complexity of the overall query and making it easier to troubleshoot.

Let's say you're building a report that shows customers, their total spending, and a classification of their spending behavior. First, you use a CTE to calculate the total spending, then apply **CASE** statements to categorize customers. Here's an example:

```sql
WITH total_spending AS (
    SELECT customer_id, SUM(total_price) AS total_spent
    FROM orders
    GROUP BY customer_id
)
SELECT ts.customer_id,
       ts.total_spent,
       CASE
           WHEN ts.total_spent >= 500 THEN 'High Value'
           WHEN ts.total_spent >= 100 THEN 'Medium Value'
           ELSE 'Low Value'
       END AS spending_category
FROM total_spending ts;
```
In this example, we first calculate the total spending for each customer in the CTE (`total_spending`), and then in the main query, we apply a **CASE** statement to categorize the customers based on their total spending. This approach breaks the logic into separate pieces, which enhances readability and makes the query easier to manage.

17. It's also worth noting that **CTEs** can help simplify queries that require **multiple joins**. For instance, when working with data spread across multiple tables, it can sometimes be difficult to keep track of which data is being aggregated or transformed. By using a CTE to pre-calculate or pre-filter parts of the query, you can write simpler, more efficient joins. Let's consider an example where you need to calculate sales by product category, and then join the results with another table to show the most recent sales date per product:

```sql
Copy
WITH sales_per_category AS (
   SELECT product_id, category_id, SUM(total_price) AS
total_sales
   FROM orders
   GROUP BY product_id, category_id
)
SELECT spc.product_id, spc.category_id, spc.total_sales,
p.product_name, MAX(o.order_date) AS most_recent_sale
FROM sales_per_category spc
JOIN products p ON spc.product_id = p.product_id
JOIN orders o ON spc.product_id = o.product_id
GROUP BY spc.product_id, spc.category_id, p.product_name;
```

In this case, the CTE (`sales_per_category`) is used to aggregate sales by product and category before joining the `products` and `orders` tables. This allows for a more concise and readable query, improving both performance and clarity, especially when dealing with complex data transformations and relationships.

18. Another important consideration when working with **CASE** statements is how they interact with **null values**. SQL evaluates NULL as an unknown value, which can sometimes result in unexpected behavior when using **CASE** statements. If your dataset contains NULL values, you should always account for them explicitly, either by using the IS NULL condition in the **CASE** statement or by substituting NULL with a default value. For example, suppose you want to categorize products based on their availability, but some products have missing availability data (represented as NULL):

```sql
Copy
SELECT product_id, product_name,
      CASE
          WHEN stock_quantity IS NULL THEN 'Unknown'
          WHEN stock_quantity > 0 THEN 'In Stock'
          ELSE 'Out of Stock'
      END AS stock_status
FROM products;
```

In this query, we explicitly handle NULL values by categorizing them as 'Unknown', ensuring that no product is left uncategorized. Handling NULL properly ensures that your query results are accurate and comprehensive, especially when your data may be incomplete or inconsistent.

19. As you continue using **CTEs** and **CASE** statements, you will encounter scenarios where combining them with other SQL functions like **aggregation**, **window functions**, and **joins** can unlock even more powerful querying capabilities. For example, by using a **window function** alongside a **CASE** statement, you can perform operations like ranking and calculating running totals while applying conditional logic to each row. Here's an example where we calculate running totals for sales, but only for orders above a certain threshold using a CASE statement within a window function:

```sql
Copy
SELECT order_id, total_price,
       SUM(CASE WHEN total_price > 100 THEN total_price
ELSE 0 END)
       OVER (ORDER BY order_date) AS running_total
FROM orders;
```

In this query, the **CASE** statement is used to include only those orders with a total price above 100 in the running total calculation. Using **window functions** with **CASE** statements allows you to perform complex analytics and conditional aggregations in a streamlined manner.

20. Another powerful use case for **CASE** and **CTEs** is in **data transformation** tasks. You can use **CASE** statements to map or translate data into different formats or categories for reporting purposes. For example, imagine you have a `sales` table with transaction statuses represented by codes like "P" for Pending, "C" for Completed, and "R" for Refunded. You can use a **CASE** statement to translate these codes into more user-friendly text in your report:

```sql
Copy
WITH status_translation AS (
  SELECT transaction_id,
         CASE status_code
           WHEN 'P' THEN 'Pending'
           WHEN 'C' THEN 'Completed'
           WHEN 'R' THEN 'Refunded'
           ELSE 'Unknown'
         END AS status_description
  FROM sales
)
SELECT transaction_id, status_description
FROM status_translation;
```

This approach allows you to easily manage data transformations without modifying the underlying data structure. By separating the transformation logic into a CTE, you can maintain a clean and efficient design for your database while still providing end users with human-readable outputs.

21. As you build increasingly complex queries, always keep in mind the performance implications of using **CASE** statements and **CTEs**. While they are powerful tools, they can sometimes introduce additional overhead, especially when working with large datasets or recursive CTEs. It's important to test and monitor the performance of your queries, particularly when you're using recursive CTEs or conditional logic that may evaluate large numbers of rows. You can optimize performance by limiting the number of rows processed in each query and ensuring that appropriate indexes are in place.

22. In conclusion, **CASE statements** and **CTEs** are essential advanced techniques that help you tackle complex data manipulation and transformation tasks in SQL. The CASE statement allows you to introduce conditional logic directly into your queries, making it easier to handle dynamic situations, categorize data, and calculate new values. **CTEs**, on the other hand, help you write more modular, readable queries by breaking complex logic into manageable parts. These techniques empower you to write powerful queries for reporting, analytics, and data transformation, allowing you to gain deeper insights from your database.

23. In the next chapter, we will dive into **window functions**, which provide a way to perform calculations across a set of rows related to the current row. These functions are widely used for running totals, moving averages, rankings, and other advanced analytical tasks. So, continue experimenting with **CASE** statements and **CTEs**, and get ready for more sophisticated SQL techniques that will take your querying skills to the next level. Happy querying!

Chapter 13: Functions and Stored Procedures

1. Welcome to one of the most powerful and practical chapters in SQL—**Functions** and **Stored Procedures**! By now, you've learned how to query and manipulate data efficiently, and you've likely realized that sometimes, you need more than just a standard SELECT statement. You need to encapsulate complex logic, improve performance, or automate repetitive tasks. That's where **functions** and **stored procedures** come in. These two features allow you to write reusable pieces of code that can be executed multiple times, making your database interactions much more efficient and maintainable. In this chapter, we'll dive deep into both **functions** and **stored procedures**, explaining their differences, their use cases, and how to create and use them.

2. Let's start with **functions**. A **function** in SQL is a predefined or user-defined routine that performs a specific task and returns a value. Functions are generally used for computations, data transformations, or validations that need to be reused across multiple queries. The main advantage of using functions is that they allow you to encapsulate complex logic into a single callable unit, making your SQL code more modular and reusable.

3. In SQL, functions are typically used in SELECT queries, WHERE clauses, or other parts of SQL statements that require a return value. The syntax for creating a basic user-defined function (UDF) is as follows:

```sql
Copy
CREATE FUNCTION function_name (parameters)
RETURNS return_type
AS
```

```
BEGIN
   -- function logic
   RETURN value;
END;
```

Let's look at an example of a function that calculates the **discounted price** for a product based on its original price and discount percentage:

sql
Copy
```sql
CREATE FUNCTION calculate_discounted_price (original_price
DECIMAL(10, 2), discount_percentage DECIMAL(5, 2))
RETURNS DECIMAL(10, 2)
AS
BEGIN
   RETURN original_price * (1 - discount_percentage / 100);
END;
```

In this example, the function `calculate_discounted_price` takes two parameters: `original_price` and `discount_percentage`. It then returns the discounted price after applying the discount.

4. Once the function is created, you can use it in your queries just like any other built-in SQL function. For example, to apply the `calculate_discounted_price` function to a list of products, you could write:

sql
Copy
```sql
SELECT product_id, product_name, original_price,
       dbo.calculate_discounted_price(original_price, 10)
AS discounted_price
FROM products;
```

This query applies the function to calculate a 10% discount for each product in the `products` table. Using functions like this allows you to centralize your logic and reuse it whenever necessary.

5. A key point to note is that functions in SQL are **deterministic** by nature. This means that, given the same input parameters, they will always return the same result. This is important for consistency and predictability, especially when you're working with complex data transformations. However, there are certain limitations to SQL functions, such as restrictions on modifying database state (e.g., you can't insert, update, or delete records inside a function). These restrictions ensure that functions remain lightweight and focused on computation.

6. Now, let's move on to **stored procedures**. A **stored procedure** is similar to a function in that it's a set of SQL statements that are stored in the database and can be executed multiple times. However, unlike functions, stored procedures do not return a value directly; instead, they are often used to perform actions like inserting, updating, or deleting data, or executing complex transactions. Stored procedures are particularly useful when you need to encapsulate a series of actions or business logic that should be executed together.

7. The syntax for creating a stored procedure is as follows:

```sql
CREATE PROCEDURE procedure_name (parameters)
AS
BEGIN
    -- stored procedure logic
END;
```

For example, let's say you want to create a stored procedure that updates the stock quantity for a product after an order is placed. The stored procedure might look like this:

```sql
CREATE PROCEDURE update_stock_quantity (IN product_id INT,
IN quantity_sold INT)
AS
BEGIN
    UPDATE products
    SET stock_quantity = stock_quantity - quantity_sold
    WHERE product_id = product_id;
END;
```

This stored procedure takes two parameters: `product_id` and `quantity_sold`. It then updates the `stock_quantity` of the product in the `products` table by subtracting the `quantity_sold`.

8. Once the stored procedure is created, you can execute it using the **EXEC** or **EXECUTE** statement:

```sql
EXEC update_stock_quantity 101, 5;
```

This will call the `update_stock_quantity` procedure, passing 101 as the `product_id` and 5 as the `quantity_sold`. Stored procedures provide an efficient way to encapsulate and automate repetitive tasks like updating stock levels, processing payments, or generating reports.

9. Stored procedures are extremely powerful because they can include multiple SQL statements, error handling, and **transaction control**. For example, if you need to update the stock quantity and also insert a record into an `order_history` table, you can include both actions in a stored procedure, ensuring that they execute as part of a single transaction. Here's an example:

sql
Copy

```sql
CREATE PROCEDURE process_order (IN product_id INT, IN
quantity INT, IN order_id INT)
AS
BEGIN
  BEGIN TRANSACTION;

  -- Update stock quantity
  UPDATE products
  SET stock_quantity = stock_quantity - quantity
  WHERE product_id = product_id;

  -- Insert into order history
  INSERT INTO order_history (order_id, product_id,
quantity)
  VALUES (order_id, product_id, quantity);

  COMMIT;
END;
```

In this case, the procedure processes the order by updating the stock quantity and recording the transaction in the `order_history` table. The use of **transactions** ensures that both actions occur together—either both succeed or both fail, maintaining data consistency.

10. Stored procedures can also take advantage of **input and output parameters**. While functions typically return a value, stored procedures can have input parameters (passed when calling the procedure) and output parameters (returned to the caller). For example, a stored procedure can calculate the total order amount and return it as an output parameter:

sql
Copy

```sql
CREATE PROCEDURE calculate_total_order_amount (IN order_id
INT, OUT total_amount DECIMAL(10, 2))
AS
BEGIN
  SELECT SUM(total_price) INTO total_amount
  FROM order_items
  WHERE order_id = order_id;
END;
```

To call this stored procedure and retrieve the output parameter, you would write:

sql
Copy

```sql
DECLARE @total DECIMAL(10, 2);
EXEC calculate_total_order_amount 101, @total OUTPUT;
SELECT @total AS total_order_amount;
```

In this example, the procedure calculates the total order amount for a given order_id, and the result is stored in the @total variable. The OUTPUT parameter allows you to pass results back from the procedure.

11. Error handling is another important feature of stored procedures. In SQL Server, for example, you can use **TRY...CATCH** blocks to handle errors gracefully. This allows you to capture errors, log them, and even roll back transactions when necessary. Here's an example:

sql
Copy

```sql
CREATE PROCEDURE safe_update_stock (IN product_id INT, IN
quantity_sold INT)
AS
BEGIN
  BEGIN TRY
    BEGIN TRANSACTION;
    UPDATE products
    SET stock_quantity = stock_quantity - quantity_sold
    WHERE product_id = product_id;
    COMMIT;
  END TRY
  BEGIN CATCH
    ROLLBACK;
    -- Handle the error (e.g., log it, rethrow it, etc.)
    PRINT 'Error occurred: ' + ERROR_MESSAGE();
  END CATCH
END;
```

In this example, the stored procedure uses **TRY...CATCH** to ensure that if an error occurs during the stock update, the transaction is rolled back, maintaining database consistency. Error handling is a critical aspect of writing robust stored procedures.

12. In conclusion, **functions** and **stored procedures** are powerful tools that enhance the flexibility, efficiency, and maintainability of your SQL code. **Functions** are perfect for encapsulating reusable logic that performs calculations or transformations and returns a value, while **stored procedures** allow you to automate complex tasks, manage transactions, and encapsulate business logic. Both can improve your workflow, reduce duplication, and centralize logic for easier maintenance.

13. In the next chapter, we will dive into **triggers**, another powerful tool for automating database operations. Triggers allow you to automatically execute SQL code in response to certain events, such as inserting, updating, or deleting data. By the end of this chapter, you'll be able to take your SQL skills to the next level with advanced automation and logic. Happy coding!

14. One important concept to remember when using **stored procedures** and **functions** is **modularity**. When creating reusable logic, it's best to keep your procedures and functions as modular as possible. For example, if you have a large piece of business logic, break it into smaller, well-defined procedures or functions that each handle a specific part of the task. This makes your code easier to manage, debug, and maintain. A large, monolithic procedure can quickly become difficult to understand and prone to errors, especially as your database evolves. By designing smaller, focused procedures and functions, you ensure that each part of your logic is self-contained and reusable across multiple queries and applications.

15. Another best practice when writing **stored procedures** and **functions** is **documenting your code**. It may seem simple now, but as your database grows and your procedures become more complex, it will be crucial to have clear documentation for each function or stored procedure. This should include information about the parameters, expected results, any side effects, and any error handling logic you've implemented. Many database management systems allow you to add comments within the code, which is an excellent way to clarify complex logic. Documenting your logic helps both you and any future developers who work with the database understand what the code is doing and why.

16. Performance optimization is another key factor to consider when working with **functions** and **stored procedures**. Both of these are powerful tools, but if not optimized properly, they can affect the overall performance of your database, especially with large datasets or complex logic. One of the most common issues is **inefficient queries** within stored procedures and functions. Always be mindful of the execution plan, especially when performing multiple joins or aggregations within a procedure. Use indexes wherever possible and avoid unnecessary calculations inside loops or recursive operations. Additionally, try to minimize the number of database calls made within the procedure—especially when dealing with large amounts of data— by using **bulk operations** or reducing the number of times you interact with the database.

17. Dynamic SQL is an incredibly powerful feature in stored procedures, allowing you to execute SQL commands that are generated on the fly. This is particularly useful when the query structure needs to vary based on user input, or when you need to execute queries with variable column names, table names, or conditions. While dynamic SQL provides flexibility, it's important to use it carefully to avoid performance issues and security risks like **SQL injection**. Always make sure that user inputs are properly sanitized and validated to prevent malicious code execution. Here's an example of using dynamic SQL inside a stored procedure to filter a query based on a column provided as input:

```sql
Copy
```

```
CREATE PROCEDURE dynamic_query_example (IN column_name
VARCHAR(50), IN value INT)
AS
BEGIN
  DECLARE @sql_query NVARCHAR(MAX);
  SET @sql_query = 'SELECT * FROM products WHERE ' +
column_name + ' = @value';
  EXEC sp_executesql @sql_query, N'@value INT', @value;
END;
```

In this example, we use `sp_executesql` to execute a dynamically constructed SQL query. The column name is passed as an argument to the procedure, allowing the query to be flexible. While dynamic SQL is useful, ensure that you validate the `column_name` input to prevent injection attacks or errors.

18. Performance tuning for stored procedures and functions is critical, especially in large databases or complex applications. As your database grows, the queries inside your procedures may take longer to execute, so it's important to consider how you can improve their performance. Here are a few tips:

- **Limit the scope of the data**: Use `WHERE` clauses to restrict the data being processed. Avoid processing unnecessary rows.

- **Use indexes wisely**: Ensure that the columns used in the `WHERE`, `JOIN`, or `ORDER BY` clauses are indexed to improve query performance.

- **Avoid complex loops**: If you're using loops inside stored procedures, try to minimize their use, as they can degrade performance. Instead, try using set-based operations, which SQL excels at.

- **Analyze execution plans**: Most DBMSs (Database Management Systems) provide tools to analyze the execution plan of your queries. Look for bottlenecks and areas that could be optimized.

An example of optimizing a stored procedure might be ensuring that operations on large datasets are done in smaller, more manageable chunks, or using **batch processing** where you perform operations in batches rather than on the entire dataset at once.

19. Another feature of **stored procedures** is **parameterized queries**. These are essential for preventing **SQL injection** attacks, a common security vulnerability where an attacker is able to manipulate the SQL query by injecting malicious SQL code. Using parameterized queries ensures that user input is treated as data rather than executable code. The example we saw earlier with `sp_executesql` demonstrates how parameters are passed safely into SQL queries.

Here's another example of parameterized SQL in a stored procedure:

```sql
Copy
CREATE PROCEDURE get_customer_orders (IN customer_id INT)
AS
BEGIN
    SELECT order_id, total_price, order_date
    FROM orders
    WHERE customer_id = @customer_id;
END;
```

In this stored procedure, the `customer_id` is passed as a parameter, ensuring that it is handled as data, not code. This prevents any form of SQL injection from happening and helps keep the database secure.

20. Versioning and **maintenance** of stored procedures and functions are also important considerations. Over time, the business logic within your database might change, requiring updates to your procedures. It's important to keep track of different versions of your stored procedures and functions. Here are some best practices for managing changes:

- **Version your procedures**: When making significant changes to a stored procedure, consider creating a new version with a different name (e.g., `update_stock_v2`) instead of overwriting the existing version. This allows you to test the new logic while keeping the old version in production.

- **Document changes**: Always document the changes you make to stored procedures. Include the reason for the change, the expected impact, and the version number.

- **Use source control**: If your database development process involves multiple developers, consider using a version control system (such as Git) to manage your stored procedures and other database objects. This ensures that changes are tracked and that you can roll back to previous versions if necessary.

21. Error handling in stored procedures is essential for ensuring smooth operation and maintaining data integrity. You can use **TRY...CATCH** blocks in SQL Server (or similar constructs in other databases) to handle errors and roll back transactions if necessary. This ensures that if an error occurs during the execution of the procedure, you can catch it, log it, and take appropriate action to maintain consistency.

Here's an example of a stored procedure with **error handling**:

```sql
Copy
CREATE PROCEDURE process_order (IN order_id INT, IN
product_id INT, IN quantity INT)
AS
BEGIN
```

```sql
BEGIN TRY
  BEGIN TRANSACTION;

    -- Update stock quantity
    UPDATE products
    SET stock_quantity = stock_quantity - quantity
    WHERE product_id = product_id;

    -- Insert into order history
    INSERT INTO order_history (order_id, product_id,
quantity)
    VALUES (order_id, product_id, quantity);

    COMMIT;
  END TRY
  BEGIN CATCH
    ROLLBACK;
    -- Log the error
    PRINT 'Error: ' + ERROR_MESSAGE();
  END CATCH
END;
```

In this example, if an error occurs during either the stock update or the insertion into the `order_history` table, the transaction is rolled back, ensuring that no partial updates are made to the database. The error message is printed for logging or debugging purposes.

22. In conclusion, **functions** and **stored procedures** are two essential tools that provide great flexibility and power in SQL. Functions help encapsulate reusable logic for computation and data transformation, while stored procedures allow you to automate processes, handle transactions, and implement complex business logic. Whether you're working on small projects or large, enterprise-level systems, learning to write efficient, modular functions and stored procedures will significantly improve your workflow, reduce redundancy, and make your database interactions more robust and secure.

23. In the next chapter, we will dive into **triggers**, another important feature in SQL that automates database actions in response to changes in data. Triggers help enforce business rules, maintain data integrity, and automate repetitive tasks. By the end of the next chapter, you will be able to create triggers that automatically react to events like inserts, updates, and deletes. So, stay tuned for more advanced SQL techniques that will help you automate and streamline your database tasks. Happy coding and optimizing!

Chapter 14: Triggers and Events

1. Welcome to Chapter 14, where we explore two of the most powerful tools in SQL for automating database tasks—**Triggers** and **Events**! These features allow you to create automatic actions that are triggered by certain database operations, such as inserting, updating, or deleting data. Triggers and events are invaluable for ensuring data integrity, enforcing business rules, and automating repetitive tasks, all while reducing the need for manual intervention. In this chapter, we'll dive deep into both, exploring what triggers and events are, when to use them, and how to create and manage them.

2. Let's start with **Triggers**. A **trigger** is a type of stored procedure that automatically executes or "fires" when certain events occur within the database. Triggers are useful for enforcing business logic, ensuring data integrity, and automating repetitive actions that need to happen every time a row is inserted, updated, or deleted. Unlike functions or stored procedures that are explicitly invoked by users, triggers are **event-driven** and happen automatically when a specified action is performed on a table or view.

3. Triggers can be set to fire in response to the following events:

- **INSERT**: Trigger fires when a new row is inserted into a table.

- **UPDATE**: Trigger fires when a row is updated in a table.

- **DELETE**: Trigger fires when a row is deleted from a table.

Triggers can also be defined as **BEFORE** or **AFTER** the event occurs:

- **BEFORE**: Trigger fires before the action (INSERT, UPDATE, DELETE) is applied.

- **AFTER**: Trigger fires after the action has been completed.

Let's look at an example of an `AFTER INSERT` trigger that logs when a new customer is added to a `customers` table:

```sql
Copy
CREATE TRIGGER log_new_customer
AFTER INSERT ON customers
FOR EACH ROW
BEGIN
  INSERT INTO customer_log (customer_id, action,
action_date)
  VALUES (NEW.customer_id, 'INSERT', NOW());
END;
```

In this example, the trigger `log_new_customer` fires **after** a new row is inserted into the `customers` table. It inserts a log entry into the `customer_log` table, recording the `customer_id`, the action (`INSERT`), and the timestamp of when the insertion occurred.

4. You can also create **BEFORE triggers** to validate or modify data before it is inserted, updated, or deleted. For example, let's say you want to ensure that a product's price is never set to a negative value before inserting a new product into the `products` table. Here's how you might create a `BEFORE INSERT` trigger for that:

```sql
Copy
CREATE TRIGGER validate_product_price
BEFORE INSERT ON products
FOR EACH ROW
BEGIN
  IF NEW.price < 0 THEN
    SIGNAL SQLSTATE '45000'
    SET MESSAGE_TEXT = 'Price cannot be negative';
  END IF;
END;
```

In this example, the trigger `validate_product_price` checks the `price` of the new product being inserted. If the price is negative, the trigger raises an error and prevents the insertion from proceeding. This type of trigger is useful for enforcing business rules and maintaining data integrity at the time of data entry.

5. One of the key benefits of triggers is their ability to automate **audit logging**. By automatically logging changes to critical data, you ensure that you have a complete record of database activity, which is especially useful for tracking changes for security or compliance purposes. For example, you can create an `AFTER UPDATE` trigger to log any changes made to the `employees` table:

```sql
Copy
CREATE TRIGGER log_employee_update
AFTER UPDATE ON employees
FOR EACH ROW
BEGIN
  INSERT INTO employee_audit_log (employee_id, old_salary,
new_salary, updated_at)
  VALUES (OLD.employee_id, OLD.salary, NEW.salary, NOW());
END;
```

This trigger fires after an employee's salary is updated, logging the old and new salary values into an `employee_audit_log` table. By using triggers for logging, you can automate the tracking of changes to sensitive data without requiring manual intervention.

6. Performance Considerations: While triggers are incredibly useful, they can impact database performance, especially if they involve complex logic or large amounts of data. Triggers are executed automatically during database operations, so if a trigger is set to fire frequently (for example, every time a record is updated), it can add overhead to the system. It's essential to ensure that triggers are efficient, limit the amount of work done inside them, and avoid complex queries or loops that could negatively affect performance. Always test the performance of your triggers and monitor their execution, especially in high-transaction environments.

7. Next, let's move on to **Events**. An **event** is a scheduled action in SQL that automatically runs at a specified time or interval. Unlike triggers, which are event-driven and respond to data changes, events are **time-driven** and are typically used for tasks like maintenance, reporting, or periodic data updates. Events are useful for automating routine tasks like cleaning up old data, generating reports, or updating statistics without requiring manual intervention.

8. In SQL, events are created using the `CREATE EVENT` statement. Here's an example of an event that deletes records from an `audit_log` table that are older than 30 days:

sql
Copy
```sql
CREATE EVENT clean_up_old_logs
ON SCHEDULE EVERY 1 DAY
STARTS '2025-01-01 00:00:00'
DO
   DELETE FROM audit_log WHERE log_date < NOW() - INTERVAL
30 DAY;
```
In this example, the event `clean_up_old_logs` runs every day, starting on January 1st, 2025. It deletes rows from the `audit_log` table that are older than 30 days. Events are an excellent way to automate maintenance tasks, freeing up valuable resources without manual intervention.

9. Events can also be used for **periodic reporting**. For instance, you could create an event that generates a daily report on sales and stores the result in a table:

sql
Copy
```sql
CREATE EVENT generate_daily_sales_report
ON SCHEDULE EVERY 1 DAY
STARTS '2025-01-01 00:00:00'
DO
   INSERT INTO daily_sales_report (report_date, total_sales)
   SELECT CURDATE(), SUM(total_price) FROM orders WHERE
order_date = CURDATE();
```
This event generates a daily sales report and stores the result in the `daily_sales_report` table, summarizing the total sales for the day. Using events for periodic reporting allows you to keep your reports up-to-date without manual intervention.

10. Event Scheduling in SQL is highly customizable. You can set the event to run at specific intervals using the `EVERY` keyword, or schedule it to start at a particular time using the `STARTS` keyword. Events can be one-time or recurring, and they can be scheduled to run at specific times of the day, such as during off-peak hours, to minimize their impact on system performance.

11. Event Management: Once events are created, they can be managed using the `SHOW EVENTS` command to view all scheduled events or `DROP EVENT` to delete events. For example, if you need to see all events in your database, you can run:

```sql
SHOW EVENTS;
```

To drop (delete) an event, you can use the `DROP EVENT` command:

```sql
DROP EVENT generate_daily_sales_report;
```

Proper event management ensures that you can track and control scheduled tasks, keeping your system organized and efficient.

12. Performance Considerations for Events: As with triggers, events can also affect performance, particularly if they are set to run frequently or perform complex operations. It's important to monitor the performance impact of scheduled events, especially if they involve large data deletions, updates, or heavy computations. Ensure that your events are optimized to minimize resource usage and are scheduled during times of low system activity, such as off-peak hours.

13. In conclusion, both **triggers** and **events** are essential tools for automating SQL tasks and improving the efficiency and consistency of your database operations. **Triggers** allow you to automate responses to specific changes in the database, ensuring that business rules and data integrity are maintained without manual intervention. **Events**, on the other hand, help automate scheduled tasks, such as maintenance and reporting, ensuring that they happen on time, every time. By mastering both triggers and events, you can build more intelligent, self-maintaining databases that handle complex tasks automatically.

14. In the next chapter, we will explore **window functions**, which are powerful tools for performing calculations across a set of rows related to the current row, allowing you to calculate running totals, ranks, moving averages, and more. Get ready to dive deeper into advanced SQL techniques! Happy automating!

15. When using **triggers**, there's one critical consideration: **trigger nesting**. Sometimes, a trigger can cause another trigger to fire, either directly or indirectly, leading to a **circular dependency**. For instance, a trigger that updates a table might inadvertently activate another trigger that performs additional modifications, leading to unintended consequences. To prevent this, many databases offer options to control trigger execution, such as **disabling triggers temporarily** or using **conditional logic** to avoid unnecessary actions. In some cases, managing trigger execution order or using flags to track whether a trigger has already been fired in a specific transaction can help prevent infinite loops or redundant actions. Understanding and managing trigger nesting is essential for maintaining the integrity of your automated processes.

16. It's also important to know that **triggers** can have a direct impact on **transaction control**. If a trigger executes within the context of a transaction, it will be part of that transaction. This means that if the trigger performs an operation that fails, it could cause the entire transaction to roll back, potentially affecting other operations. Therefore, when designing triggers, especially those that interact with critical business logic or financial transactions, you should carefully evaluate the risk of failures and ensure appropriate error handling is in place. For example, in an `AFTER UPDATE` trigger that logs changes, you might want to use `TRY...CATCH` logic to capture any errors without rolling back the original update.

17. Event Management is also crucial for optimizing your database performance, especially in production environments. Events that run at high frequencies, or during peak system load times, can impact your database's responsiveness. One common best practice is to schedule less-critical events during **off-peak hours**. For example, maintenance tasks like archiving old records, cleaning up log files, or recalculating summary data can be scheduled at night when the system experiences lower traffic. By carefully planning the timing of your events, you can avoid unnecessary system strain during busy periods.

18. Another **security consideration** when working with **triggers** and **events** is ensuring that only authorized users can create, modify, or delete them. Since these objects can perform important and potentially sensitive operations on your data, controlling access to triggers and events is essential for preventing unauthorized modifications. Use proper **role-based access control (RBAC)** to restrict access to these features and ensure that only trusted users have the ability to set up or modify triggers and events. Additionally, logging and auditing access to triggers and events helps you maintain accountability for any changes made to them.

19. In terms of **best practices**, here are a few essential guidelines when working with triggers and events:

- **Keep triggers simple and focused**: Triggers should perform a small, specific task (like logging changes or enforcing data integrity) and should not include complex logic. If a task requires complex logic, consider creating a stored procedure and calling it from the trigger.

- **Limit the number of triggers per table**: Having too many triggers on a single table can lead to performance problems and confusion over which trigger is responsible for a particular action. Be mindful of the complexity and interactions between triggers.

- **Test triggers and events thoroughly**: Always test the behavior of your triggers and events in a development or staging environment before deploying them to production. Ensure that they perform as expected without introducing performance issues or causing unexpected behavior.

- **Use transaction management carefully**: For triggers that involve multiple steps (like inserting into several tables or updating multiple rows), use **transaction control** to ensure all steps either succeed or fail as a group, maintaining data consistency.

20. In conclusion, **triggers** and **events** are powerful tools that can significantly enhance the automation, integrity, and efficiency of your database operations. Triggers allow you to automatically enforce rules and respond to changes within the database, while events enable you to automate routine tasks based on time intervals. These features are particularly useful in environments where complex business logic needs to be automated, data integrity needs to be maintained, or routine maintenance tasks need to run without human intervention. However, careful design, monitoring, and management are essential to avoid potential pitfalls such as performance degradation, unintentional loops, and security issues.

21. In the next chapter, we will explore **window functions** in SQL, which allow you to perform calculations across a set of rows that are related to the current row, such as running totals, ranking, and more. These advanced analytical functions open up a wide range of possibilities for performing sophisticated data analysis with ease. Get ready to dive into another essential feature of SQL that can enhance your ability to perform complex queries! Happy automating with triggers and events!

Chapter 15: Working with Views

1. Welcome to Chapter 15, where we delve into the powerful concept of **Views**! A **view** is essentially a virtual table in SQL that allows you to simplify complex queries by encapsulating them into a single object. By creating a view, you can encapsulate select logic and reuse it across your database without the need to repeatedly write the same query. Views are essential for organizing and abstracting your data, improving security by restricting access to specific columns or rows, and providing a cleaner, more manageable way of working with your data. In this chapter, we will explore the creation, management, and best practices for working with views in SQL.

2. Let's start by defining what a **view** is. A view is a stored query that acts as a **virtual table**. Unlike a regular table, a view does not store data on its own. Instead, it **queries** data from one or more underlying tables and presents it as if it were a single table. When you query a view, you are essentially querying the result of the stored SELECT statement that defines the view.

For example, suppose you want to create a simplified version of a customer order report that only includes customer names and their total order amounts. Instead of writing a long query each time you need this report, you could create a view to simplify the process. Here's how you might create such a view:

sql
Copy
```
CREATE VIEW customer_order_summary AS
SELECT c.customer_id, c.first_name, c.last_name,
SUM(o.total_price) AS total_spent
```

```sql
FROM customers c
JOIN orders o ON c.customer_id = o.customer_id
GROUP BY c.customer_id, c.first_name, c.last_name;
```
In this example, the `customer_order_summary` view is defined by joining the `customers` and `orders` tables and calculating the total amount spent by each customer. The result of this query is stored in the view, and now you can access it like a regular table.

3. To query data from a view, you simply use a `SELECT` statement:

sql
Copy
```sql
SELECT * FROM customer_order_summary;
```
This retrieves the customer names and their corresponding total order amounts from the view. Behind the scenes, SQL executes the stored query of the view each time you query it, so the results are always up-to-date.

4. One of the primary benefits of using views is **abstraction**. By creating views, you can simplify complex queries, abstract away the underlying table structures, and present only the necessary data to users or applications. This is especially useful when dealing with databases with many tables or when you want to hide certain details from end users. For instance, you can create a view that joins several tables to provide a simplified, user-friendly version of the data without exposing the complexity of the underlying tables.

Let's consider a scenario where you have multiple tables for `orders`, `order_items`, and `products`. You might want to create a view that aggregates sales data for reporting purposes:

sql
Copy
```sql
CREATE VIEW sales_report AS
SELECT o.order_id, o.order_date, p.product_name,
oi.quantity, oi.price, (oi.quantity * oi.price) AS
total_price
FROM orders o
JOIN order_items oi ON o.order_id = oi.order_id
JOIN products p ON oi.product_id = p.product_id;
```
This view provides a clear, consolidated sales report from multiple tables, with product names, quantities, and total prices, abstracting away the complexities of the underlying data.

5. Views also help with **security** by allowing you to control which data users can access. Instead of granting direct access to sensitive tables, you can create views that expose only the necessary columns or rows. This is particularly useful in multi-user environments where you want to restrict access to specific information. For instance, instead of allowing users to directly query the `employees` table, you could create a view that only shows employee names and positions:

```sql
Copy
CREATE VIEW employee_name_position AS
SELECT first_name, last_name, position
FROM employees;
```

Users who need access to employee names and positions can query this view, while the underlying sensitive data (such as salaries or personal details) remains hidden. Views allow you to provide **role-based access control** to your data.

6. Views are also useful for **data aggregation**. If you frequently need to perform the same aggregations across multiple tables, such as calculating total sales per region or average order value, you can store these aggregate queries in a view to simplify reporting. For example, if you need to calculate the total sales for each region, you can create a view like this:

```sql
Copy
CREATE VIEW regional_sales_summary AS
SELECT region, SUM(total_price) AS total_sales
FROM orders
GROUP BY region;
```

Now, whenever you need to report on regional sales, you can simply query the `regional_sales_summary` view without having to write the SUM and GROUP BY logic repeatedly.

7. It's also important to note that views can be **updatable**, meaning you can use them in INSERT, UPDATE, and DELETE operations just like a regular table. However, not all views are updatable. Views are updatable if:

- They are based on a single table.

- They do not include aggregate functions (SUM, AVG, etc.) or DISTINCT.

- They do not involve complex joins or subqueries.

For example, if you create a simple view that pulls data from a single table without any aggregation, you can perform INSERT, UPDATE, or DELETE operations on it directly:

```sql
Copy
CREATE VIEW simple_customer_view AS
SELECT customer_id, first_name, last_name
FROM customers;

UPDATE simple_customer_view
```

```sql
SET first_name = 'John'
WHERE customer_id = 1;
```
This query updates the `first_name` of the customer with `customer_id` 1 using the `simple_customer_view`. However, if your view involves complex logic or multiple tables, it may not be directly updatable.

8. If you need a **non-updatable view** or want to **restrict** the ability to update the data through the view, you can define the view to include only read-only operations, often for reporting or data retrieval purposes. This ensures that users can query the data without modifying it, preserving data integrity.

9. Materialized Views are a special type of view that stores the result of the query physically on the disk. Unlike standard views, which are virtual and are re-executed every time they are queried, materialized views store the result of the query at the time of creation or refresh. This makes them much faster for read-heavy operations, as the data is already pre-computed.

For example, a materialized view for sales data might be refreshed every night to speed up reporting during the day:

sql
Copy
```sql
CREATE MATERIALIZED VIEW daily_sales_summary AS
SELECT region, SUM(total_price) AS total_sales
FROM orders
GROUP BY region;
```
Materialized views are especially useful in data warehouses and reporting systems, where you need fast access to pre-computed data but can afford to refresh the view periodically rather than in real-time.

10. Managing Views involves using commands to view, alter, or drop existing views. For example, you can use `SHOW VIEWS` to see a list of all views in your database:

sql
Copy
```sql
SHOW VIEWS;
```
To modify an existing view, you typically need to drop and recreate it. SQL doesn't have a direct `ALTER VIEW` command for changing an existing view, so you need to use `DROP VIEW` and then create a new one with the updated logic:

sql
Copy
```sql
DROP VIEW customer_order_summary;
CREATE VIEW customer_order_summary AS
```

```sql
SELECT c.customer_id, c.first_name, c.last_name,
SUM(o.total_price) AS total_spent
FROM customers c
JOIN orders o ON c.customer_id = o.customer_id
GROUP BY c.customer_id, c.first_name, c.last_name;
```

To drop a view, use the DROP VIEW statement:

sql
Copy

```sql
DROP VIEW customer_order_summary;
```

11. In conclusion, **views** are a highly useful feature in SQL that allow you to encapsulate complex queries, improve security, simplify reporting, and enforce data integrity. They are particularly effective for simplifying queries, restricting access to sensitive data, and abstracting away complex relationships between tables. By creating and managing views, you can streamline your workflow, increase efficiency, and provide a more secure and modular approach to interacting with your database.

12. In the next chapter, we will explore **window functions**, which allow you to perform complex calculations across a set of rows related to the current row. These functions are particularly useful for running totals, rankings, and advanced analytics. With window functions, you'll be able to perform sophisticated data analysis with much less complexity. So, get ready for more advanced techniques to level up your SQL skills! Happy querying!

13. As we discussed earlier, **views** are incredibly powerful for simplifying complex queries and abstracting data access. However, it's important to understand the limitations and performance implications of using views, especially in large databases with complex structures. While views can help you reduce redundancy and improve query readability, poorly designed views or overusing them can have a negative impact on performance. When a view is queried, the database engine must execute the underlying query each time, which can slow down query performance, particularly with large datasets or complex joins.

14. One common performance consideration is the **nested views** scenario. Sometimes, views can be nested within other views, leading to multiple layers of queries being executed. While this can be useful for modularizing query logic, it can also result in slower performance due to the cascading effects of querying multiple views. It's essential to test the performance of nested views and be mindful of the added complexity. In cases where performance becomes an issue, you may need to optimize the views or consider other options, like using materialized views (which store the query result) or simplifying the query logic.

15. Another performance concern is the **complexity of the SELECT statements** used within views. Views are ideal for abstracting away complex joins and aggregations, but if the underlying queries are very complex or involve large amounts of data, the view can become a bottleneck. One way to mitigate this is to break up the query into smaller, more efficient parts. If necessary, optimize the underlying query by adding indexes to columns that are frequently used in joins or filters. Additionally, always ensure that views are only used when they provide clear benefits in terms of maintainability and performance.

16. While **views** provide a convenient way to simplify data access and ensure consistency, you must consider **how and when** to refresh or recreate views, especially if the underlying tables undergo frequent changes. For example, when a table's schema is modified (columns added or removed), the view may become invalid or return incorrect results. In some cases, you may need to **drop and recreate** views when changes to the underlying tables are made, but this can be cumbersome if done frequently. In such cases, you might want to adopt a **version control system** for your views, so changes to the underlying data model are tracked, and any required updates to views are handled consistently.

17. It's also worth mentioning that **views** can be used in combination with **user-defined functions (UDFs)** to create more complex data transformation logic. You can use UDFs to perform custom calculations or transformations on data, and then incorporate those functions into your views. This approach allows you to keep your views focused on data retrieval while offloading more complex logic to reusable functions. Here's an example where a custom function is used to format product prices before displaying them in a view:

sql
Copy
```sql
CREATE FUNCTION format_price (price DECIMAL(10, 2))
RETURNS VARCHAR(20)
BEGIN
   RETURN CONCAT('$', FORMAT(price, 2));
END;
```
You can then use this function in your view definition:

sql
Copy
```sql
CREATE VIEW product_price_view AS
SELECT product_id, product_name, dbo.format_price(price) AS
formatted_price
FROM products;
```
This approach allows you to modularize and reuse your logic across multiple views or queries, keeping your SQL code clean and maintainable.

18. Indexes are another important consideration when working with views. If you're using views frequently in queries, it's a good idea to make sure that the underlying tables are indexed properly, particularly the columns involved in joins, filters, and sorting. However, views themselves cannot have indexes directly applied to them. Instead, indexing the underlying tables efficiently can help improve the performance of queries that use the views. In addition, consider **materialized views** if performance is a significant concern, especially for read-heavy applications, since materialized views store the results of the query and can be refreshed periodically.

19. It's also important to understand how **views** interact with **transactions**. When querying a view within a transaction, any updates to the underlying data will not be reflected in the view until the transaction is committed, which can sometimes lead to inconsistent results in a long-running transaction. If you need real-time data consistency, make sure your transactions are kept short and that views are not being queried within long or complex transactions that modify data frequently. Additionally, ensure that your transaction isolation levels are appropriate to prevent issues like **dirty reads** or **phantom reads** when working with views.

20. Finally, it's essential to understand the impact of **views on database schema design**. While views provide great flexibility in querying data, they should not be used as a substitute for proper database normalization and schema design. It's important to understand that views are a tool for simplifying and abstracting complex queries; they are not a solution for poorly designed database schemas. Make sure your database tables are well-normalized, and use views to simplify access to the data without compromising the underlying data structure.

21. In conclusion, **views** are an invaluable tool for simplifying complex SQL queries, abstracting data access, and improving the maintainability of your SQL code. By allowing you to encapsulate complex joins, filters, and aggregations, views help make your queries more readable and modular. However, it's important to use views wisely and be aware of their performance implications, especially when working with large datasets or complex queries. Proper indexing, modular design, and careful management of views can help ensure that they provide the intended benefits while avoiding performance bottlenecks.

22. In the next chapter, we will dive into **window functions**—another advanced feature that allows you to perform calculations across sets of rows that are related to the current row. Window functions are particularly useful for advanced reporting tasks like running totals, rankings, and moving averages. So, get ready to enhance your analytical SQL skills with this powerful feature. Happy querying with views!

Chapter 16: Data Security and Permissions

1. Welcome to Chapter 16, where we dive into an incredibly important topic in the world of databases—**Data Security and Permissions**! Data security is critical to safeguarding your database from unauthorized access, modifications, and potential data breaches. SQL provides a wide array of tools and techniques to ensure that only authorized users can access, modify, or manage specific parts of your database. This chapter will cover the basics of data security in SQL, focusing on user management, roles, permissions, and best practices for securing your database. By the end of this chapter, you'll have a solid understanding of how to enforce security policies in SQL to protect your sensitive data.

2. Let's begin by discussing the **fundamentals of database security**. In SQL, security is enforced primarily through **authentication** and **authorization**. **Authentication** refers to the process of verifying the identity of a user trying to access the database, typically through a **username** and **password**. Once authenticated, **authorization** ensures that the user has the necessary permissions to perform specific actions on the database, such as reading, writing, or modifying data.

Authentication and authorization work together to ensure that only authorized users can access sensitive data. For example, when a user logs into the database, the system checks their credentials (authentication). Once authenticated, the system checks what actions the user is allowed to perform based on their assigned **roles** and **permissions** (authorization).

3. User Management in SQL is the process of creating, managing, and maintaining user accounts in your database system. SQL provides commands for creating users, altering their properties, and removing them when no longer needed. The basic syntax to create a user in SQL looks like this:

sql
Copy

```sql
CREATE USER 'username' IDENTIFIED BY 'password';
```

For example, to create a user named `jdoe` with the password `mypassword`, you would run:

sql
Copy

```sql
CREATE USER 'jdoe' IDENTIFIED BY 'mypassword';
```

Once the user is created, you can assign them **roles** or **permissions** to define what actions they can perform within the database.

4. Roles are a fundamental part of SQL security. A role is a collection of permissions that can be granted to one or more users. Rather than assigning permissions directly to individual users, roles allow you to manage security more efficiently by grouping related permissions. For example, a **DBA** (Database Administrator) role might have permissions to read, write, and modify data, while a **readonly** role might only have permission to read data from tables.

You can create a role using the following syntax:

sql
Copy

```sql
CREATE ROLE role_name;
```

To assign a role to a user, you use the **GRANT** statement:

sql
Copy

```sql
GRANT role_name TO username;
```

For example, to grant the `readonly` role to the user `jdoe`, you would run:

sql
Copy

```sql
GRANT readonly TO jdoe;
```

This ensures that `jdoe` only has read-only access to the database, reducing the risk of accidental data modifications.

5. Permissions in SQL define the actions a user can perform on specific objects in the database, such as tables, views, or stored procedures. Common permissions include:

- **SELECT**: Allows the user to read data from a table.

- **INSERT**: Allows the user to add new rows to a table.

- **UPDATE**: Allows the user to modify existing data in a table.

- **DELETE**: Allows the user to delete data from a table.

- **EXECUTE**: Allows the user to execute stored procedures or functions.

Permissions can be granted directly to users or through roles. For example, to grant a user `jdoe` permission to read data from the `customers` table, you would run:

sql
Copy
```
GRANT SELECT ON customers TO jdoe;
```
You can also revoke permissions if needed:

sql
Copy
```
REVOKE SELECT ON customers FROM jdoe;
```
This flexibility allows you to fine-tune access to sensitive data based on the principle of **least privilege**, ensuring users only have access to the data they need to do their job.

6. Granular Permissions are useful when you want to limit access to specific columns or rows within a table. While SQL doesn't support column-level or row-level permissions natively in every database system, you can implement them in a few ways. One common approach is to **create views** that expose only specific columns or rows to users, effectively controlling what data they can access.

For example, if you have a table of employees but don't want certain users to access salary data, you can create a view that excludes this sensitive information:

sql
Copy
```
CREATE VIEW employee_view AS
SELECT employee_id, first_name, last_name, position
FROM employees;
```
Now, you can grant users permission to query the `employee_view` without giving them access to the full `employees` table, ensuring sensitive data (like salaries) remains protected.

7. Row-Level Security (RLS) allows you to define access policies based on the content of individual rows in a table. This feature is particularly useful when you need to limit access based on user-specific conditions, such as ensuring that a user can only access data relevant to their department or region. For example, you might want to allow each regional manager to access only the data for their region.

SQL Server and PostgreSQL, among others, provide native support for **Row-Level Security**. For instance, in PostgreSQL, you could define a policy that ensures users can only access rows where the `region` column matches their assigned region:

sql
Copy
```sql
CREATE POLICY region_policy
ON employees
FOR SELECT
USING (region = current_user);
```
This policy ensures that each user can only query data from their specific region. Row-level security adds an extra layer of control over data access and is essential when working with sensitive, user-specific data.

8. Audit Logs are an essential part of database security. They provide a trail of actions taken by users within the database, helping you detect unauthorized access, track changes to sensitive data, and maintain compliance with regulations. Many database systems provide tools for creating audit logs that record actions such as `SELECT`, `INSERT`, `UPDATE`, and `DELETE` operations.

For example, you can create triggers that automatically log changes to a table:

sql
Copy
```sql
CREATE TRIGGER audit_changes
AFTER INSERT OR UPDATE OR DELETE ON customers
FOR EACH ROW
BEGIN
   INSERT INTO audit_log (operation, table_name, record_id,
old_data, new_data, changed_at)
   VALUES (TG_OP, 'customers', OLD.customer_id, OLD.*,
NEW.*, NOW());
END;
```
This trigger captures any `INSERT`, `UPDATE`, or `DELETE` operations on the `customers` table and logs the changes in an `audit_log` table. You can then query the `audit_log` to track user activities and identify potential security issues.

9. Data Encryption is a key aspect of database security, ensuring that sensitive data is protected from unauthorized access. SQL provides options for **encrypting** data at rest (stored data) and in transit (data being transmitted over a network). **Transparent Data Encryption (TDE)** is commonly used to encrypt data at rest, while **SSL/TLS** encryption can be used to encrypt data in transit.

For example, if you're using **SSL/TLS** encryption for a MySQL database, you can configure the connection to encrypt all data sent between the database server and clients, preventing eavesdropping on sensitive information like passwords and personal details.

10. Backup Security is often overlooked but is a critical component of database security. Regular backups are essential to protect against data loss, but it's equally important to ensure that backups are properly secured. Backup files contain a complete copy of your database and, if not protected, can be accessed by unauthorized individuals.

To secure backups, consider encrypting backup files and storing them in secure, access-controlled locations. Ensure that only authorized users have access to backup files, and regularly test your backup and restoration procedures to ensure that your data is recoverable in the event of a disaster.

11. Best Practices for Database Security:

- **Use strong passwords** for database users, and require password changes periodically.

- **Limit user privileges** using the principle of least privilege, ensuring users have only the necessary permissions.

- **Monitor database activity** by implementing audit logs and setting up alerts for suspicious activity.

- **Encrypt sensitive data**, both at rest and in transit, to protect it from unauthorized access.

- **Regularly back up** your database and secure backup files.

- **Use multi-factor authentication (MFA)** for database access, especially for administrative accounts.

- **Regularly patch** your database system to protect against vulnerabilities.

12. In conclusion, **data security** and **permissions** are critical to maintaining the integrity and confidentiality of your database. By implementing user management, assigning roles and permissions, controlling access to sensitive data, and employing encryption and audit logging, you can safeguard your database from unauthorized access and potential breaches. Following these best practices ensures that your database remains secure, compliant with regulations, and protected from malicious actors.

13. In the next chapter, we will explore **advanced SQL optimization techniques** to help you fine-tune your queries and improve the performance of your database. This will include indexing strategies, query optimization, and how to analyze and resolve performance bottlenecks. Get ready to boost your SQL skills to the next level! Happy securing your database!

14. As part of your ongoing security strategy, it's essential to understand the concept of **privilege escalation**. This occurs when a user gains access to privileges they should not have, often due to improper role assignments or configuration errors. Privilege escalation can be accidental or malicious, but regardless of the cause, it can lead to serious security risks. To prevent privilege escalation, ensure that user roles and permissions are clearly defined and reviewed regularly. Use **audit logs** to track any changes to roles or permissions and quickly detect any unauthorized modifications. Additionally, implement **access control lists (ACLs)** and make sure that only authorized users can modify roles or permissions.

15. Database Auditing is another critical area of database security. Auditing provides an ongoing way to monitor user activity and ensures that all actions performed in the database are traceable. Most database management systems (DBMS) allow you to enable auditing features to track who is accessing the database, what operations they are performing, and when these actions take place. You can audit a variety of database activities, including login attempts, SELECT, INSERT, UPDATE, DELETE commands, and changes to the database schema or permissions. For example, in MySQL, you can use the `AUDIT` plugin to enable auditing capabilities, or in SQL Server, you can enable **SQL Server Audit** to track and log user actions.

It's important to review audit logs regularly for suspicious activities, such as unusual access patterns or unauthorized queries. By keeping a close eye on database activity, you can quickly detect and mitigate potential security threats. Additionally, setting up **alerts** based on certain actions (like the creation of new users or changes to sensitive data) can help ensure timely responses to security incidents.

16. When dealing with **external access** to your database, ensure that access is tightly controlled. If your database is accessed from outside your corporate network, use **firewalls, VPNs,** and **SSH** to secure the connection. For instance, in cloud environments, databases often need to be exposed to external services, but it's critical to configure proper firewall rules, ensuring that only trusted IPs can communicate with the database. Always use **encrypted connections** (SSL/TLS) to ensure that data transmitted between the client and the server is protected from interception.

17. Another important consideration for external access is **database tunneling**. Database tunneling allows you to securely access a database over the internet by encrypting the data sent over the network, often via an intermediary server. When setting up a tunnel, make sure that the database connection is authenticated properly, and the tunnel is closed when not in use to avoid leaving an open security gap. Only allow specific users to create and manage tunnels to ensure unauthorized individuals don't have unrestricted access to your database.

18. It's also a good idea to periodically **review your security posture**. This includes testing the strength of your database security measures by performing **penetration testing** and running **security audits**. Penetration testing involves simulating attacks on your database to identify vulnerabilities that hackers might exploit. You can also conduct vulnerability scans using security tools designed to identify weaknesses in your SQL database configuration, outdated software versions, and potential misconfigurations that may expose your data to risks.

19. Backup Security is often overlooked but is one of the most critical aspects of database security. Your backup files contain all of your data, and if an attacker gains access to them, they could compromise your entire system. Always encrypt backup files and store them in a **secure, off-site location** to prevent unauthorized access. Consider using cloud storage providers that offer built-in security features, like **encryption** and **access control** to store backups securely. Additionally, regularly test your backup restoration procedures to ensure that in case of a disaster, you can recover your data in a timely manner without data corruption or loss.

20. When securing your database, **data masking** can be a helpful technique, especially for development and testing environments. Data masking involves replacing sensitive data with fictional but realistic values to protect privacy while maintaining the usability of the data. For example, you can mask customer names, social security numbers, or financial information in non-production environments to prevent accidental exposure while still allowing your developers and testers to work with realistic datasets.

There are several tools and techniques available for **dynamic data masking** in SQL Server and other DBMS systems. This allows you to apply masking rules to specific columns and make sure that sensitive data is only visible to those with the necessary privileges. By using data masking, you can reduce the risk of exposing sensitive information to unauthorized individuals while still enabling productive work in your database environments.

21. Security Patches are essential to keep your database system secure. Database vendors regularly release updates and patches to fix known vulnerabilities or improve security. Make sure you keep your DBMS up-to-date with the latest patches to protect your system from known exploits. It's important to regularly check for **security updates** and apply them as part of your regular maintenance cycle. To ensure that critical patches are applied in a timely manner, automate patch management wherever possible and test patches in a staging environment before deploying them to production.

22. In conclusion, **data security and permissions** are critical elements of maintaining a safe and efficient database system. By implementing strong **authentication** mechanisms, defining clear **roles and permissions**, and utilizing advanced security features like encryption, auditing, and secure backup practices, you can protect your data from unauthorized access, breaches, and potential data loss. A proactive approach to managing user access—by following the principle of **least privilege**—ensures that users only have the minimum necessary permissions to perform their tasks, significantly reducing the risk of accidental or malicious changes to your database.

Additionally, using **role-based access control (RBAC)** allows you to organize users into well-defined roles, ensuring that each user has access to only the data that they need. This greatly simplifies user management and enhances security. Regularly reviewing your database's security policies, access logs, and configurations, as well as testing for vulnerabilities, will help you maintain a resilient security posture and stay ahead of potential threats.

23. It's also essential to adopt a **comprehensive security strategy** that incorporates data security into every phase of database management. From data encryption at rest and in transit, to monitoring and auditing user activity, your database security plan should be multi-faceted and adaptable to evolving security threats. This also means educating and training staff to follow best security practices, as human error remains one of the most common causes of data breaches.

As you move forward, be sure to test your security measures regularly, stay informed about the latest threats, and make necessary adjustments to your database security protocols. Always back up your data, and ensure that backups are also properly secured and regularly tested for integrity.

24. In the next chapter, we will delve into **advanced SQL optimization techniques** that will allow you to fine-tune your queries and database performance. These techniques include indexing strategies, query optimization, and how to identify and resolve performance bottlenecks. Mastering these concepts will enable you to manage large-scale databases with high performance and efficiency, ensuring that your system can handle complex operations quickly and without downtime. Prepare to enhance your SQL expertise even further as we explore the world of performance tuning and query optimization. Happy securing your database, and here's to optimizing your queries to the next level!

Chapter 17: Transactions and Isolation Levels

1. Welcome to Chapter 17! In this chapter, we'll dive into the important concept of **transactions** and **isolation levels**—two core elements in SQL that help ensure data consistency, reliability, and proper handling of concurrent operations. As your database grows and multiple users or processes interact with it simultaneously, ensuring that operations are executed in a way that maintains data integrity becomes crucial. **Transactions** and **isolation levels** are the foundation of this process, allowing you to control how changes to the database are handled, committed, and isolated from other operations. By the end of this chapter, you'll have a solid understanding of how to manage data transactions and handle concurrency effectively in your SQL environment.

2. Let's start by exploring **Atomicity** in greater detail. **Atomicity** ensures that a transaction is treated as a single unit, which means either all of its operations are completed successfully, or none of them are. This is often referred to as the **"all-or-nothing"** principle. For instance, in a bank transfer between two accounts, you would never want the money to be deducted from one account without being credited to the other. If one part of the transaction succeeds but the other fails, the entire transaction must be rolled back to maintain consistency in the database.

To see this in action, consider a money transfer between two accounts:

```sql
Copy
BEGIN TRANSACTION;
UPDATE account SET balance = balance - 100 WHERE account_id = 1;
UPDATE account SET balance = balance + 100 WHERE account_id = 2;
COMMIT;
```

If the UPDATE for the second account fails (say, due to insufficient funds or a system error), the entire transaction will fail, and the balances of both accounts will remain unchanged. This ensures that the database remains consistent, and partial transactions are never committed.

3. Consistency is the next key principle in ACID compliance. It ensures that a transaction takes the database from one valid state to another. A consistent database is one that adheres to all the rules, constraints, and triggers defined within it. For example, if a database schema has a constraint that the balance of a bank account cannot be negative, consistency ensures that no transaction will violate this rule. If a transaction would violate a constraint, the transaction is rolled back, and the database remains in its original state.

For instance, if we try to transfer money from one account but the `balance` constraint is violated, such as attempting to withdraw more than the available balance, the transaction would be rolled back, preserving the consistency of the database:

sql
Copy
```
BEGIN TRANSACTION;
UPDATE account SET balance = balance - 100 WHERE account_id
= 1;
UPDATE account SET balance = balance + 100 WHERE account_id
= 2;
-- Assuming the balance of account 1 is less than 100
COMMIT;  -- This will fail due to consistency violation and
rollback.
```
Here, the violation of the consistency rule would cause the system to reject the operation and keep the database in a valid state.

4. Isolation is another essential concept that helps maintain the integrity of transactions, especially when multiple transactions are being processed concurrently. It dictates how the operations in one transaction are isolated from other concurrent transactions. Without proper isolation, transactions could interfere with one another, leading to issues like dirty reads, non-repeatable reads, and phantom reads.

SQL databases provide various **isolation levels**, each of which defines the level of visibility one transaction has to the data being manipulated by other concurrent transactions. The isolation level can significantly affect both the performance and consistency of your database.

Let's briefly look at the isolation levels we discussed earlier:

- **Read Uncommitted** allows for dirty reads.

- **Read Committed** ensures that a transaction only reads committed data.

- **Repeatable Read** ensures that data read during a transaction cannot change, but still allows for phantom reads.

- **Serializable** ensures the highest level of isolation, preventing dirty reads, non-repeatable reads, and phantom reads.

5. Each isolation level brings a trade-off between **performance** and **data consistency**. The more isolated a transaction is, the fewer resources are shared with other concurrent transactions, but this can lead to **blocking** and decreased system throughput. On the other hand, reducing the level of isolation allows more concurrent operations, but increases the risk of reading inconsistent or outdated data. Deciding on the appropriate isolation level depends on the nature of the application and the specific transaction requirements.

For example, in a banking application, you might choose **Serializable** isolation to ensure that no two users can simultaneously transfer money from the same account, while for a report-generating system, **Read Committed** might be sufficient, as some level of data staleness might be acceptable for performance reasons.

6. The final ACID property is **Durability**, which ensures that once a transaction is committed, its changes are permanent and will survive any subsequent system crashes or failures. The database guarantees that once the COMMIT command is issued, the transaction's changes will be saved to the database and won't be lost, even if the system crashes immediately afterward.

For example, in the case of an online shopping platform, once a customer's order has been confirmed and a transaction is committed, the database ensures that this order data remains intact, even if the server crashes or experiences a power failure shortly thereafter. This is achieved through mechanisms like transaction logs and **write-ahead logging (WAL)**.

7. The concept of **transaction logs** ties into Durability. Every change made by a transaction is first written to a transaction log before the actual changes are made to the database. This log helps the database maintain durability and recover from crashes. In the event of a failure, the database can use the transaction log to roll back incomplete transactions or reapply committed transactions, ensuring that no data is lost. Many modern database systems have robust logging systems in place to support this, and understanding how transaction logs work is key to ensuring durability and recovery.

8. One important aspect of working with transactions is understanding the **impact of concurrency** and how transactions are executed in environments with multiple users or applications. When multiple transactions are occurring simultaneously, conflicts can arise, leading to issues like deadlocks or performance degradation.

A **deadlock** happens when two or more transactions are waiting on each other to release resources, causing them to be stuck indefinitely. Database systems usually have mechanisms to detect deadlocks, and they will automatically choose to roll back one of the transactions to resolve the deadlock. Here's a simplified example:

- Transaction A locks resource X and waits for resource Y.

- Transaction B locks resource Y and waits for resource X.

To prevent deadlocks, make sure that your transactions acquire locks in a consistent order, and avoid holding locks for extended periods of time. In some cases, using **optimistic concurrency**

control (OCC) can help reduce the likelihood of conflicts, especially when the system can tolerate occasional conflicts.

9. In high-concurrency environments, it's also important to consider **lock contention**, which happens when multiple transactions try to access the same data simultaneously. This can lead to **lock waits**, where a transaction must wait for another to release a lock before it can proceed. You can minimize lock contention by:

- **Indexing** columns used in queries to reduce the amount of data being locked.

- Using **shorter transactions** to minimize the time locks are held.

- Applying **appropriate isolation levels** to balance consistency with performance.

10. To summarize, **transactions** and **isolation levels** play a crucial role in ensuring that your database remains consistent, reliable, and efficient in a multi-user environment. By using **ACID properties**, such as **atomicity**, **consistency**, **isolation**, and **durability**, you can create transactions that handle errors and system crashes gracefully. Meanwhile, choosing the right **isolation level** for your use case will help you balance data consistency with the need for concurrency and performance.

11. In the next chapter, we will discuss **advanced SQL optimization techniques** to help you fine-tune your queries and database performance. These techniques will include strategies for indexing, query optimization, and how to diagnose and resolve performance bottlenecks. By mastering these concepts, you will be able to handle large-scale databases with greater efficiency and ensure that your system remains fast and responsive as it grows. Get ready to dive deeper into SQL performance optimization! Happy transacting!

12. Now that we've covered the core concepts of transactions and isolation levels, it's important to dive a little deeper into **deadlock resolution**. While most modern database systems can automatically detect and resolve deadlocks by **terminating one of the involved transactions**, this can have significant implications depending on which transaction is chosen for termination. Typically, the system will choose to roll back the transaction that has done the least amount of work (i.e., the one that has locked the fewest resources), but this may not always align with your business priorities.

To prevent deadlocks, one effective approach is to **minimize the duration** of transactions. The longer a transaction holds locks on data, the more likely it is to conflict with others. By reducing the scope of the transaction and limiting the number of resources it locks, you can reduce the risk of deadlocks. Also, **order consistency**—ensuring that transactions always acquire locks on resources in the same order—can prevent cyclical dependencies that lead to deadlocks.

13. Another useful technique for improving transaction concurrency and reducing locking contention is **optimistic concurrency control (OCC)**. Instead of locking data when reading it, OCC assumes that conflicts are rare and only checks for conflicts when committing the transaction. If another transaction has modified the data you are working with in the meantime, the system will abort your transaction, and you can choose to retry it. OCC is highly effective in environments where write conflicts are infrequent but needs to be carefully managed to avoid the overhead of retries.

14. Transaction Size and Efficiency are another important consideration. The larger a transaction is, the more data it touches and the longer it will take to complete. This can cause performance issues, particularly in high-concurrency environments where multiple transactions are competing for database resources. A good practice is to keep transactions as small and efficient as possible by:

- Breaking larger transactions into smaller ones.

- Using **batch processing** to handle large amounts of data in smaller chunks.

- Avoiding unnecessary updates and focusing only on the rows or records that need modification.

Additionally, avoid **long-running transactions**. The longer a transaction runs, the longer locks will be held, which can lead to blocking and other performance problems. Shorter transactions also improve the chances of detecting conflicts earlier, thus reducing the risk of deadlocks and improving concurrency.

15. It's also important to understand **transaction logs** and their role in maintaining database integrity. Every operation that is part of a transaction is logged in a **transaction log**. This log records every change made to the database, allowing the system to roll back a transaction if necessary, and ensures **durability** (the "D" in ACID). In the event of a crash or power failure, the transaction log allows the database to replay committed transactions and recover to a consistent state.

Transaction logs also play a critical role in **replication** and **backup recovery**. In systems that support **point-in-time recovery (PITR)**, transaction logs allow you to restore your database to the exact state it was in at a specific moment. Regular backups combined with transaction logs give you a powerful tool for disaster recovery.

16. Concurrency Control is essential when dealing with multiple transactions trying to access the same data simultaneously. In SQL, **locking** mechanisms are used to control access to data. There are different types of locks:

- **Shared Locks**: These locks allow multiple transactions to read data but prevent any transaction from modifying the data.

- **Exclusive Locks**: These locks prevent other transactions from reading or modifying the data.

- **Update Locks**: These locks are used to prevent deadlocks during updates by allowing a transaction to hold a lock while updating data.

SQL uses **lock escalation** to manage resources efficiently. When a transaction locks too many rows, the database may escalate the lock to a table-level lock to improve performance. However, this can also reduce concurrency, so it's important to balance lock granularity and the number of locks held at any given time.

17. Another factor that impacts transaction performance is **network latency**. For distributed databases or applications that require remote database access, network latency can significantly affect the speed at which transactions are executed. When transactions are dependent on remote database resources, network delays can cause timeouts, slow down transaction commits, and increase the chance of deadlocks.

To mitigate network latency:

- Use **caching** for frequently accessed data to reduce the number of database queries.

- Ensure your database and application are **geographically close** to reduce round-trip latency.

- Optimize transaction sizes to reduce the time spent over the network.

18. Multi-Version Concurrency Control (MVCC) is a concurrency control method used by many modern database systems (such as PostgreSQL and MySQL's InnoDB). MVCC allows multiple transactions to access the same data without directly interfering with each other by providing each transaction with a snapshot of the database at the time the transaction started. This approach avoids locking the data and ensures that transactions can run concurrently without conflicts.

MVCC provides **high concurrency** and avoids many of the issues associated with locking mechanisms, but it can also introduce additional complexity in terms of managing and cleaning up **old versions** of data. Regular **vacuuming** or **garbage collection** is required to remove these obsolete data versions.

19. Transaction Management Best Practices include:

- **Begin transactions only when needed**: Avoid opening transactions too early or keeping them open longer than necessary.

- **Use appropriate isolation levels**: Choose the isolation level that strikes a balance between concurrency and consistency. For instance, use **Read Committed** in situations where you need to avoid dirty reads but can tolerate non-repeatable reads.

- **Use explicit locking**: If needed, use explicit locking (e.g., `SELECT FOR UPDATE`) to ensure that only one transaction can access a row or table at a time.

- **Avoid nested transactions**: Nested transactions can lead to complexity and can result in unintended rollbacks if inner transactions fail.

- **Always handle errors**: Use proper error handling and ensure that **ROLLBACK** is used if something goes wrong during the transaction.

20. In conclusion, **transactions** and **isolation levels** are fundamental concepts that ensure your database operations are reliable, consistent, and efficient. By understanding how to manage transactions and choose the right isolation level, you can avoid common concurrency issues like deadlocks, dirty reads, and non-repeatable reads. Additionally, implementing proper transaction management practices can help you achieve a good balance between data consistency and high system performance.

21. In the next chapter, we will dive into **advanced SQL optimization techniques**, where we'll explore indexing strategies, query optimization, and methods to improve overall database performance. With these tools, you'll be able to write more efficient SQL queries and design databases that can handle even the most demanding workloads. Get ready to enhance your SQL skills and take your performance tuning to the next level! Happy transacting and optimizing!

Chapter 18: Advanced Join Techniques: Self-Joins and Cross Joins

1. Welcome to Chapter 18! In this chapter, we will explore two advanced **join techniques** in SQL: **Self-Joins** and **Cross Joins**. While you may already be familiar with standard joins like **INNER JOIN** and **LEFT JOIN**, these two techniques take SQL's ability to combine data to the next level. They allow for more complex data relationships, which can be critical for specific queries that involve hierarchical data or need to perform calculations across all combinations of rows. By the end of this chapter, you'll understand when and how to use **Self-Joins** and **Cross Joins** to solve more challenging data problems and make your SQL queries more versatile and efficient.

2. Let's start with the concept of a **Self-Join**. A **Self-Join** is a type of join where a table is joined with itself. While this may sound unusual, it's extremely useful for situations where you need to compare rows within the same table. For example, in an employee database, you may want to find relationships between employees and their managers, but both employees and managers are stored in the same table.

To perform a **Self-Join**, we treat the same table as if it were two separate tables by **aliasing** the table. Here's an example with an `employees` table, where each employee has a `manager_id` that refers to the `employee_id` of their manager:

```sql
Copy
SELECT e1.employee_id, e1.name AS employee_name, e2.name AS manager_name
FROM employees e1
JOIN employees e2 ON e1.manager_id = e2.employee_id;
```

In this query, we are joining the `employees` table with itself. We alias the first instance of the `employees` table as `e1` (for employee) and the second instance as `e2` (for manager). The JOIN condition is `e1.manager_id = e2.employee_id`, meaning we are linking each employee to their corresponding manager. The result would show each employee alongside their manager's name.

3. Self-Joins are often used when you need to work with hierarchical data. For example, in an organizational chart, you may want to list employees with their direct managers or retrieve employees who work under the same manager. You can also use **Self-Joins** to find relationships between other data that resides in the same table, such as comparing product prices or finding duplicate entries in a list of items.

For instance, to find employees who have the same manager, you can use a Self-Join like this:

sql
Copy
```sql
SELECT e1.employee_id, e1.name, e2.name AS peer_name
FROM employees e1
JOIN employees e2 ON e1.manager_id = e2.manager_id
WHERE e1.employee_id != e2.employee_id;
```
This query lists all pairs of employees who share the same manager. By joining `e1` and `e2` on the `manager_id` column, and adding the condition `e1.employee_id != e2.employee_id`, we ensure that we're not matching an employee to themselves.

4. Cross Joins are another advanced join technique, and they are quite different from the typical **INNER JOIN** or **LEFT JOIN** you may have used. A **Cross Join** (also known as a **Cartesian Join**) combines every row from the first table with every row from the second table, producing the **Cartesian product** of the two sets. It does not require a ON condition, unlike other joins. Because of this, a **Cross Join** can result in a large number of rows if both tables contain many rows.

For example, if you have a `colors` table and a `sizes` table:

sql
Copy
```sql
SELECT * FROM colors;
```

color
Red
Green
Blue

sql
Copy
```sql
SELECT * FROM sizes;
```

size
Small
Medium

Large

A **Cross Join** between these two tables would produce a result like this:

```sql
Copy
SELECT color, size FROM colors
CROSS JOIN sizes;
```

color	size
Red	Small
Red	Medium
Red	Large
Green	Small
Green	Medium
Green	Large
Blue	Small
Blue	Medium
Blue	Large

This results in every combination of `color` and `size`. In this case, you get 9 combinations, as there are 3 rows in each table (3 colors and 3 sizes). Cross Joins are useful when you need to generate combinations of data, like creating a list of all possible pairs between two sets, generating sample data, or modeling scenarios that require every possible combination.

5. One important thing to keep in mind when using **Cross Joins** is that they can result in **very large result sets**. If one of the tables has 1,000 rows and the other has 500, a Cross Join would produce 500,000 rows (1,000 x 500). Be cautious when using Cross Joins on large tables, as they can lead to performance issues due to the sheer size of the result set. It's essential to make sure you really need the Cartesian product before using this join type.

6. Practical Applications of Cross Joins: Cross Joins are commonly used for scenarios like generating **combinations**, **pairing** data, or **creating matrix-like results**. For example, in a product and price list, a Cross Join might be used to create all possible combinations of products and regions for a sales report, where each product is available in each region. You might also use a Cross Join to create a list of every possible combination of **date** and **time** for a schedule, to ensure that no time slot is missing from your scheduling system.

7. When using a **Self-Join**, one common pitfall is not properly aliasing your tables, which can lead to confusion and incorrect query results. When joining a table with itself, always make sure to use distinct aliases for each instance of the table, as we did earlier with `e1` and `e2`. If you omit aliases, SQL won't know which table to refer to, and this can result in errors or unexpected results.

8. Similarly, when using a **Cross Join**, ensure you are aware of the potentially large dataset you're generating. This is especially important when using **Cross Joins** on tables that contain a large number of rows, such as user or transaction tables. Be aware of how many rows the Cross Join will produce and whether you can handle that volume of data within your application.

9. To recap, **Self-Joins** are an essential tool for comparing rows within the same table, especially when working with hierarchical data or identifying relationships between rows. You can use Self-Joins to model relationships such as employee-manager pairs, or find items that are related to one another in the same table. **Cross Joins**, on the other hand, generate the Cartesian product of two sets, producing every combination of rows from both tables. This technique is great for generating combinations, testing, or building reports that require all possible pairs of data, but should be used cautiously due to the potential for large result sets.

10. In conclusion, these two advanced join techniques—**Self-Joins** and **Cross Joins**—open up a world of possibilities for working with data in SQL. Whether you're comparing rows within a table, building complex relationships, or generating all possible combinations of two data sets, mastering these join types will enhance your SQL querying capabilities.

11. In the next chapter, we will explore **advanced subqueries**, which allow you to use queries within other queries to create even more powerful and flexible SQL statements. Subqueries are an essential tool for building complex queries that depend on dynamic data and need to be executed multiple times within a single query. Get ready to dive deeper into advanced SQL techniques! Happy joining!

12. When working with **Self-Joins**, there are a few additional scenarios where this technique becomes even more valuable. A **Self-Join** is especially useful when you need to find **hierarchical relationships** within a table. Consider a **categories** table that organizes products into different levels of a hierarchy, such as subcategories and parent categories. A Self-Join allows you to retrieve both parent and child categories in the same query.

Here's an example where we want to list each category alongside its parent category:

sql
Copy
```sql
CREATE TABLE categories (
    category_id INT PRIMARY KEY,
    category_name VARCHAR(100),
    parent_category_id INT
);
```

```sql
SELECT c1.category_name AS subcategory, c2.category_name AS
parent_category
FROM categories c1
LEFT JOIN categories c2 ON c1.parent_category_id =
c2.category_id;
```
In this case, we use a **LEFT JOIN** to get all categories, including those without a parent (i.e., root categories). By joining `categories` to itself, we get each category along with the name of its parent category, if available. This kind of query is often used to represent tree-like structures or hierarchies within a single table.

13. Another advanced application of **Self-Joins** can be in identifying **duplicates** in your data. For instance, if you have a `customers` table with names, email addresses, and phone numbers, you can use a Self-Join to find customers who have the same email address or phone number. Here's an example of how to find duplicate email addresses in a `customers` table:

sql
Copy
```sql
SELECT c1.customer_id, c1.email
FROM customers c1
JOIN customers c2 ON c1.email = c2.email
WHERE c1.customer_id != c2.customer_id;
```
This query checks for customers who share the same email address but have different `customer_id`s. The condition `c1.customer_id != c2.customer_id` ensures that we're not matching a record to itself. By using a Self-Join, you can identify potential duplicate entries in your database.

14. Moving on to **Cross Joins**, these are incredibly useful for generating combinations of data, but they should be used cautiously. **Cross Joins** create all possible combinations of rows from both tables, so they can generate very large result sets. One practical example of using a **Cross Join** is for generating **combinations of time slots** for scheduling purposes. For instance, let's say you have a table of **days** and a table of **available times** for meetings. A **Cross Join** allows you to list every possible day and time combination:

sql
Copy
```sql
CREATE TABLE days (
    day_name VARCHAR(50)
);

CREATE TABLE times (
    time_slot VARCHAR(50)
);
```

```sql
SELECT d.day_name, t.time_slot
FROM days d
CROSS JOIN times t;
```

If the `days` table has 7 rows (representing the days of the week) and the `times` table has 3 rows (representing different time slots), the result will be 21 combinations (7 x 3). This type of query is useful for creating schedules, availability calendars, or generating combinations for testing.

15. Another useful application of a **Cross Join** is when you need to perform **cartesian product-based analysis** or generate large sets of test data. For instance, imagine you need to analyze every possible combination of product prices and customer segments in a marketing campaign. You could create a **Cross Join** between a table of product prices and a table of customer segments to model all possible scenarios:

sql
Copy
```sql
CREATE TABLE product_prices (
    product_name VARCHAR(100),
    price DECIMAL(10, 2)
);

CREATE TABLE customer_segments (
    segment_name VARCHAR(100)
);

SELECT p.product_name, p.price, c.segment_name
FROM product_prices p
CROSS JOIN customer_segments c;
```

This will produce a combination of every product with every customer segment, which could be used for analysis or testing various marketing strategies.

16. Another application of **Cross Joins** is when you need to generate **combinations for statistical analysis**. For instance, in scenarios like calculating **pairwise comparisons** or testing different combinations of factors, a Cross Join can be used to generate all possible combinations of the two sets involved. Let's say you have a table of **products** and a table of **discount percentages**, and you want to calculate the total price for each product at each discount level. Using a Cross Join allows you to quickly generate every possible product-discount combination:

sql
Copy
```sql
CREATE TABLE products (
    product_id INT,
    product_name VARCHAR(100),
```

```
    price DECIMAL(10, 2)
);

CREATE TABLE discounts (
    discount_percentage INT
);

SELECT p.product_name, p.price, d.discount_percentage,
       p.price * (1 - d.discount_percentage / 100.0) AS
discounted_price
FROM products p
CROSS JOIN discounts d;
```
In this case, the Cross Join generates every combination of product and discount percentage, and we calculate the discounted price for each combination. This is a great way to perform **what-if analysis**, where you want to test different scenarios or combinations to see how they affect your results.

17. One often overlooked feature of **Cross Joins** is their use in **data expansion**. Sometimes you may have a dataset that needs to be expanded to include additional combinations. For example, if you're generating combinations of product types and delivery regions for a logistics company, you might use a Cross Join to ensure that all combinations of products and regions are covered, even if some of them do not exist yet. By generating all combinations first, you can later filter out the ones that don't apply or have zero stock, for instance.

18. As useful as **Cross Joins** and **Self-Joins** can be, it's important to be cautious about their performance implications. Both join types can produce large result sets, particularly with **Cross Joins**, where the result set grows exponentially. When working with Cross Joins, it's essential to consider:

- **Limit the number of rows**: Always be mindful of how many rows your Cross Join will generate. If you only need a subset of the combinations, apply a **WHERE** clause or **LIMIT** to restrict the output.

- **Ensure relevant indexes**: For Self-Joins, ensure that the columns used for joining are indexed to improve query performance. For Cross Joins, the performance impact may be less influenced by indexing, but it's still important to optimize the underlying tables where possible.

19. Self-Joins, on the other hand, are generally less resource-intensive than Cross Joins but still require careful design. When performing a Self-Join, consider breaking down your logic into multiple steps if necessary, especially if the table you're working with is large or if the join condition is complex. You may also want to use **temporary tables** to hold intermediate results before joining them together, which can improve performance in certain situations.

20. A useful practice when working with **Self-Joins** is to ensure that you **optimize the join condition**. For example, if you're using a Self-Join to compare dates within the same table, make sure that your join condition doesn't unnecessarily increase the result set size. Using **date ranges** or more precise filtering within the join condition can reduce the number of rows processed and improve query performance.

21. In conclusion, **Self-Joins** and **Cross Joins** are invaluable tools when you need to work with complex relationships within your data. A **Self-Join** allows you to compare rows within the same table, which is useful for tasks such as finding hierarchical relationships, comparing records, and detecting duplicates. A **Cross Join**, though more powerful and potentially more computationally expensive, enables you to generate all possible combinations of data, making it ideal for scenarios like data testing, statistical analysis, and exploratory data analysis.

While these join techniques can significantly enhance your SQL querying capabilities, it's important to always consider the **size** of the result sets they generate and their **performance implications**. By using these joins wisely and ensuring that the data they operate on is well-indexed, you can unlock the full potential of your database for complex analytical tasks.

22. In the next chapter, we will explore **advanced subqueries**, which provide a method for performing queries within other queries. Subqueries are incredibly powerful for breaking down complex tasks and allowing dynamic filtering, calculation, or transformation of data. They can simplify your SQL code and provide flexibility when dealing with multiple datasets within a single query. Get ready to dive deeper into SQL with advanced subquery techniques! Happy joining and querying!

Chapter 19: Query Optimization and Execution Plans

1. Welcome to Chapter 19! In this chapter, we'll explore one of the most critical skills for any SQL developer—**query optimization**. As your databases grow and your queries become more complex, you'll inevitably face situations where queries take longer to execute than expected. This chapter will teach you how to diagnose and resolve performance bottlenecks by understanding **execution plans**, optimizing your queries, and applying best practices for ensuring fast, efficient SQL queries. By the end of this chapter, you'll be well-equipped to tackle performance issues and make your SQL queries run like a well-oiled machine.

2. Let's start with the concept of **query optimization**. In simple terms, query optimization is the process of improving the performance of a SQL query by reducing its execution time and resource consumption. Query optimization involves a combination of techniques, including:

- Writing efficient SQL code.

- Using **indexes** effectively.

- Understanding the **execution plan** of a query.

- Applying the appropriate **join strategies**.

- Avoiding costly operations like **nested queries** or inefficient **subqueries**.

Ultimately, the goal of query optimization is to make sure that your database responds quickly to requests, especially as data volume and complexity increase.

3. One of the first tools you'll need for optimization is the **execution plan**. The **execution plan** shows you how SQL Server (or any other database engine) intends to execute your query. It's essentially a roadmap of the steps that the database will take to retrieve the results of the query, including how it joins tables, accesses indexes, and handles data. The execution plan can reveal inefficiencies such as full table scans, missing indexes, or unnecessary sorting.

To see the execution plan for a query in SQL Server, you can simply add the `EXPLAIN` keyword before your query or use SQL Server's **Query Analyzer** to display the plan. For example:

sql
Copy
```
EXPLAIN SELECT * FROM employees WHERE department_id = 5;
```
This will return the execution plan, which outlines how the database engine will execute the query, including whether it will use an index, perform a table scan, or use a nested loop join.

4. Understanding the **execution plan** is critical for identifying and resolving performance issues. The plan will include operations like:

- **Table Scans**: If the database engine has to scan an entire table to find the relevant rows, it can be very slow, especially on large tables.

- **Index Scans**: Index scans are faster than full table scans but can still be costly if the index isn't optimal for the query.

- **Joins**: The execution plan will tell you how the database is performing joins (e.g., nested loop join, hash join, merge join).

- **Sort Operations**: If your query requires sorting, this can often be an expensive operation, particularly on large datasets.

- **Aggregations**: Calculating aggregates like `SUM()`, `COUNT()`, or `AVG()` can be resource-intensive, especially when there are a lot of rows involved.

By reviewing the execution plan, you can spot inefficiencies and adjust your query accordingly to improve performance.

5. Indexing is one of the most powerful techniques for speeding up query performance. Indexes are data structures that improve the speed of data retrieval operations. When a query is run, the database engine can use indexes to quickly locate the rows that match the query criteria, rather than performing a full table scan. However, it's important to note that while indexes speed up query performance, they can slow down data modification operations like `INSERT`, `UPDATE`, and `DELETE`, as the index itself needs to be updated.

The key to effective indexing is to index the right columns—those that are used frequently in `WHERE` clauses, `JOIN` conditions, or `ORDER BY` clauses. For example, if you often query a `customers` table by `last_name`, it would make sense to create an index on the `last_name` column:

sql
Copy
```sql
CREATE INDEX idx_last_name ON customers(last_name);
```
Be sure to analyze your execution plan after adding indexes to ensure they are being used effectively. SQL Server, for instance, might use an index for some queries but still perform a full table scan in cases where the query doesn't align well with the indexed columns.

6. Avoiding Full Table Scans: Full table scans are generally the slowest form of querying data, as they involve reading the entire table to find matching rows. You can minimize full table scans by ensuring that:

- Your queries are **well-indexed** on the columns used in the `WHERE` clause.

- You use **selectivity**: queries that filter on columns with high cardinality (many unique values) are more likely to benefit from indexing.

- You avoid using **wildcards** at the beginning of a search string in `LIKE` queries, which can prevent the database from using indexes effectively. For example:

sql
Copy
```sql
-- This query will result in a full table scan
SELECT * FROM products WHERE product_name LIKE '%widget';
```
This query will not be able to take advantage of an index on the `product_name` column because the wildcard `%` appears at the beginning of the string. If possible, avoid this kind of pattern and try to use the wildcard at the end, where it can still benefit from indexing.

7. Join Optimization: Joins are one of the most common sources of performance issues. The execution plan will show you how the database is performing the join—whether it's using a nested loop join, a hash join, or a merge join. Different join types are suited to different kinds of data, and understanding which one is being used can help you optimize your queries.

- **Nested Loop Joins**: These are ideal when one of the tables is small or when the result of the first table is small. They can be inefficient on large datasets.

- **Hash Joins**: These are used when the tables being joined are large and there's no index on the join column. Hash joins can be slower when the tables involved are very large.

- **Merge Joins**: These are efficient when both tables being joined are sorted on the join key or can be efficiently sorted. Merge joins require fewer resources than nested loop or hash joins on large datasets.

To optimize joins, consider the following strategies:

- Ensure that join columns are indexed.

- Use **INNER JOIN** over **LEFT JOIN** when possible, as it tends to perform better, especially when you don't need the extra rows that a `LEFT JOIN` might return.

- Avoid **CROSS JOINS** unless absolutely necessary, as they generate the Cartesian product, which can result in an exponentially large result set.

8. Query Refactoring is another important technique in query optimization. Even well-written queries can sometimes be inefficient due to how the logic is structured. You can optimize queries by refactoring them to:

- Eliminate unnecessary subqueries: Replace them with **JOINs** or **CTEs** (Common Table Expressions) to improve readability and performance.

- Remove unnecessary columns: Always select only the columns you need. Using `SELECT *` returns all columns, which can be slow when dealing with large tables.

- Use **aggregations efficiently**: If you need to aggregate large datasets, consider breaking the task into smaller parts or using indexed views.

Here's an example of refactoring a query with a subquery into a more efficient query with a join:

```sql
Copy
-- Inefficient query with subquery
SELECT order_id, (SELECT MAX(order_date) FROM orders WHERE
customer_id = o.customer_id)
FROM orders o;

-- Optimized query with JOIN
SELECT o.order_id, MAX(o.order_date) AS latest_order_date
FROM orders o
GROUP BY o.customer_id;
```

In this case, the original query uses a correlated subquery, which can be inefficient. The refactored query replaces the subquery with an aggregate function (**MAX**), improving readability and performance.

9. Common Performance Bottlenecks:

- *SELECT :* Always specify the exact columns you need, rather than using `SELECT *`. This minimizes the amount of data retrieved, improving performance.

- **Large Transactions:** Large transactions can lead to locking and resource contention, so break them into smaller transactions if possible.

- **Implicit Conversions:** Avoid implicit data type conversions, as they can slow down queries. For example, comparing a string to a number can cause the database to convert data types, which can result in performance hits.

10. In conclusion, optimizing SQL queries is both an art and a science. By understanding and interpreting the **execution plan**, applying proper **indexing strategies**, optimizing **joins**, and refactoring queries, you can significantly improve your query performance. Regularly monitoring and optimizing your queries will ensure that your database remains efficient, even as your data grows.

11. In the next chapter, we will explore **advanced indexing strategies**, where we will go deeper into how to leverage indexing to improve query performance and how to avoid common pitfalls. Understanding indexing techniques is crucial for building highly responsive databases. Get ready to fine-tune your database and take your optimization skills to the next level! Happy optimizing!

12. As we've discussed, **execution plans** are key to diagnosing performance bottlenecks, but knowing how to interpret them is equally important. The **execution plan** tells you how SQL Server (or another database management system) will execute a query. A well-understood execution plan will reveal:

- **Table scans** (which are usually slow, as the entire table is read),

- **Index scans** or **seeks** (which are faster because the database engine looks only at relevant portions of the data),

- The type of **join** being performed, and

- Whether the **optimizer** is choosing the most efficient plan.

When reviewing an execution plan, pay special attention to **expensive operations** that consume the most resources (CPU, memory, I/O). These are often displayed as **"cost"** percentages, which can help pinpoint which part of the query needs optimization. In general, you'll want to avoid **full table scans** and large sorts, and ensure that your joins are optimized. If the execution plan shows **table scans** on large tables, consider adding or improving indexes on the columns used in the `WHERE`, `JOIN`, or `ORDER BY` clauses.

13. Analyzing Query Performance using tools like **SQL Profiler** or **Query Store** in SQL Server can help you track slow-running queries over time and identify patterns. You can also use **Execution Plan Caching** to observe how often SQL Server chooses to recompile a query. By analyzing repeated executions of the same query and their corresponding execution plans, you can get a better sense of where optimizations are needed.

14. Another tool to improve query performance is **parameterization**. Parameterized queries are precompiled by the database engine, which means the SQL engine does not have to parse and compile the query each time it's executed. This can reduce CPU usage and increase the efficiency of your queries. Parameterized queries also protect against **SQL injection** attacks, providing an additional layer of security. Here's an example of a parameterized query:

```sql
Copy
SELECT * FROM customers WHERE last_name = @last_name;
```

In this query, `@last_name` is a parameter, and the query is sent to the database engine with a **plan** that is reused each time the query is executed. This can significantly improve performance, especially in situations where the same query is executed frequently with different parameters.

15. Batching is another optimization technique worth mentioning. When working with large datasets, rather than executing one large query that affects thousands of rows, consider breaking the operation into smaller **batches**. This helps reduce the load on the database and minimizes locking issues. For example, when updating records in a large table, you could process them in chunks, which prevents the system from locking the entire table and improves throughput.

Here's an example of updating records in batches:

```sql
Copy
DECLARE @BatchSize INT = 1000;
DECLARE @Offset INT = 0;

WHILE (1 = 1)
BEGIN
    UPDATE TOP (@BatchSize) orders
    SET order_status = 'Processed'
    WHERE order_status = 'Pending'
    AND order_id > @Offset;

    SET @Offset = (SELECT MAX(order_id) FROM orders WHERE
order_status = 'Pending');

    IF @@ROWCOUNT < @BatchSize
        BREAK;
END
```

In this case, the query updates records in batches of 1000, preventing excessive locking and ensuring the database doesn't get overwhelmed with large updates.

16. Materialized Views can also be a powerful optimization tool. A **materialized view** is a precomputed query result stored as a physical table, as opposed to a regular view that is computed on the fly every time it is queried. Materialized views can significantly improve performance for complex aggregate queries, especially when the data doesn't change frequently. The downside is that materialized views need to be **refreshed** periodically to ensure they reflect the most recent data.

Here's an example of a materialized view to store precomputed sales totals by region:

sql
Copy
```
CREATE MATERIALIZED VIEW regional_sales_summary AS
SELECT region, SUM(total_sales) AS total_sales
FROM sales
GROUP BY region;
```
This query stores the result of the aggregation, allowing you to access the summarized data without having to compute it on the fly every time. Periodically, you would refresh the materialized view to ensure it's up-to-date with the latest sales data.

17. Another essential technique in **query optimization** is the use of **Covering Indexes**. A **covering index** is an index that includes all the columns needed for a query, meaning that the query can be satisfied entirely by the index itself without having to access the underlying table. This can be particularly helpful for improving performance on **SELECT** queries that frequently retrieve the same set of columns.

For example, if you frequently query the `orders` table to get `order_id`, `order_date`, and `customer_id`, you could create a covering index on these columns:

sql
Copy
```
CREATE INDEX idx_orders_covering ON orders(order_id,
order_date, customer_id);
```
With a covering index, the database engine doesn't have to access the `orders` table at all, and the query can be served directly from the index, making the retrieval much faster.

18. Denormalization is a technique that can sometimes improve query performance, especially in read-heavy applications. In **denormalization**, data from multiple tables is combined into a single table, reducing the need for joins. While this can improve read performance, it comes at the cost of increased redundancy and potential for data inconsistencies. Use denormalization carefully and only when you're sure that the benefits outweigh the drawbacks.

For example, if you frequently join two large tables to retrieve customer information and order details, denormalizing the tables into a single customer-order table may reduce the need for costly joins:

sql
Copy

```
CREATE TABLE customer_orders AS
SELECT c.customer_id, c.first_name, c.last_name,
o.order_id, o.order_date
FROM customers c
JOIN orders o ON c.customer_id = o.customer_id;
```
This denormalized table allows you to query customer orders without needing to join the `customers` and `orders` tables. However, you would need to handle data integrity manually to ensure the tables stay in sync when data changes.

19. A common mistake in query optimization is **over-indexing**. While indexes can significantly speed up queries, creating too many indexes can actually hurt performance, especially for **write operations** (INSERT, UPDATE, DELETE). Each time data is modified, all relevant indexes need to be updated, which can lead to significant overhead. Therefore, it's essential to strike a balance and index only the columns that are frequently queried and essential for performance.

A good strategy is to:

- **Monitor query patterns**: Regularly analyze which queries are being executed most frequently and optimize them.

- **Prioritize indexing**: Focus on indexing columns used in joins, filters (`WHERE`), or sorting (`ORDER BY`), as these will provide the greatest performance benefit.

- **Avoid redundant indexes**: If you have multiple indexes that cover the same columns or combinations of columns, they may be unnecessary.

20. Query Caching is another method of improving performance for frequently executed queries. Query caching stores the results of a query so that if the same query is run again, the database can return the cached result instead of recalculating it. Caching can be a major performance booster, especially for complex queries that do not change often. However, the cache must be updated when the underlying data changes.

For example, SQL Server provides **Query Store**, which can track and store query plans and execution statistics. By using **Query Store**, you can analyze performance regressions over time and identify areas where optimizations may be needed.

21. In conclusion, **query optimization** is a critical aspect of maintaining fast, scalable databases. By understanding execution plans, using indexes wisely, and applying techniques like batch processing, materialized views, denormalization, and query caching, you can ensure that your SQL queries perform efficiently—even as data grows. Query optimization is an ongoing process that requires regular monitoring, analysis, and adjustments based on evolving use cases.

22. In the next chapter, we will explore **advanced indexing strategies**, where we'll dive deeper into how indexes work and how to optimize them for different types of queries. Understanding indexing is fundamental for writing fast queries, especially as your database grows. Get ready to take your query optimization skills to the next level! Happy optimizing!

Chapter 20: Working with Large Datasets

1. Welcome to Chapter 20, where we'll dive into one of the most important challenges SQL developers face—**working with large datasets**. As your databases grow, performance issues inevitably arise, and the need to handle large volumes of data efficiently becomes more critical than ever. In this chapter, we'll discuss the strategies and techniques you can use to optimize query performance, manage resources, and ensure that your SQL operations remain fast and scalable. Whether you're dealing with billions of rows in a table or running complex reports on massive datasets, this chapter will help you manage big data effectively.

2. The first step in handling large datasets is understanding the importance of **efficient data retrieval**. As your datasets grow, the time it takes to retrieve data can increase exponentially if you don't optimize your queries properly. For instance, performing a `SELECT *` on a table with millions of rows can cause significant strain on the system. Instead, you should always aim to query **only the data you need**, using more specific column selections and **filters** to reduce the number of rows being retrieved.

For example:

sql
Copy
```sql
-- Inefficient: retrieves all columns and rows
SELECT * FROM large_table;

-- Efficient: retrieves only specific columns and rows
SELECT column1, column2 FROM large_table WHERE column3 = 'some_value';
```
The more specific your query, the less data needs to be read from the database, which can significantly improve performance.

3. Another key to working with large datasets is **indexing**. Proper use of indexes can speed up data retrieval dramatically. Indexes allow the database engine to quickly locate rows based on specific column values, reducing the need for full table scans. However, it's important to use indexes judiciously. Over-indexing can lead to performance issues, especially during `INSERT`, `UPDATE`, and `DELETE` operations, because the index itself needs to be updated.

When indexing large datasets, prioritize columns that are frequently used in `WHERE` clauses, `JOIN` conditions, or `ORDER BY` clauses. For example, in a large `sales` table, if you frequently filter by `order_date` or `product_id`, it would make sense to create indexes on those columns:

sql
Copy
```sql
CREATE INDEX idx_order_date ON sales(order_date);
CREATE INDEX idx_product_id ON sales(product_id);
```

Ensure that the indexes are being used by analyzing the **execution plan** of your queries, and avoid unnecessary indexes that may slow down write operations.

4. Partitioning is another technique that can help you manage large datasets effectively. Partitioning divides a large table into smaller, more manageable pieces called **partitions**, based on a key column. For example, you could partition a `sales` table by `order_date`, with each partition representing data for a specific year or month. Partitioning allows the database to operate on smaller subsets of the data, improving query performance and maintenance operations.

For example, here's how you might partition a table based on a date range:

sql
Copy
```sql
CREATE TABLE sales (
    order_id INT,
    order_date DATE,
    amount DECIMAL(10, 2)
) PARTITION BY RANGE (YEAR(order_date)) (
    PARTITION p_2020 VALUES LESS THAN (2021),
    PARTITION p_2021 VALUES LESS THAN (2022),
    PARTITION p_2022 VALUES LESS THAN (2023)
);
```
With partitioning, queries that filter on `order_date` can be faster, as the database engine only needs to scan the relevant partition rather than the entire table.

5. Data Archiving is a critical strategy for managing large datasets. Over time, some data becomes less relevant or is accessed infrequently. Archiving allows you to move older data to a separate table or database, which keeps your active dataset smaller and improves performance.

For example, in a `transactions` table, you might archive transactions older than five years into a separate table:

sql
Copy
```sql
-- Move old transactions to the archive table
INSERT INTO transactions_archive
SELECT * FROM transactions WHERE transaction_date <
'2018-01-01';


-- Delete archived data from the main table
DELETE FROM transactions WHERE transaction_date <
'2018-01-01';
```
By archiving older data, you ensure that your queries are focused on the most relevant, up-to-date information, reducing the load on your main operational database.

6. When working with large datasets, **batch processing** is often an essential technique. Instead of running one massive query that affects thousands or millions of rows, it's better to break the task into smaller, more manageable pieces. For example, when updating records in a large table, you can process them in batches to avoid locking the entire table and to reduce the overall impact on performance.

Here's an example of how you might update a large number of rows in batches:

```sql
DECLARE @BatchSize INT = 1000;
DECLARE @Offset INT = 0;

WHILE (1 = 1)
BEGIN
    UPDATE TOP (@BatchSize) orders
    SET order_status = 'Shipped'
    WHERE order_status = 'Pending'
    AND order_id > @Offset;

    SET @Offset = (SELECT MAX(order_id) FROM orders WHERE
order_status = 'Pending');

    IF @@ROWCOUNT < @BatchSize
        BREAK;
END
```

By processing the updates in batches, you reduce the risk of **locking contention** and allow other operations to run without being blocked by the update process.

7. Query Parallelism is another technique that can improve the performance of queries on large datasets. Some databases, like SQL Server and PostgreSQL, allow you to leverage **parallel query execution**. This means the database can break a large query into smaller subqueries and run them in parallel, using multiple CPU cores. This can drastically reduce the time required to execute complex queries.

To enable parallelism, ensure that your database configuration allows it, and use appropriate **query hints** or **optimizations** to ensure the query can be split into parallel tasks. For example, in SQL Server, the MAXDOP query hint can be used to limit the number of CPU cores used in parallel queries:

```sql
SELECT * FROM large_table
OPTION (MAXDOP 4);
```

This would allow the query to use a maximum of 4 CPU cores for parallel execution.

8. Compression is a powerful tool for working with large datasets, especially when dealing with tables that store large text or binary data. Compression reduces the size of the data stored on disk and can improve I/O performance. Many modern databases, including SQL Server and PostgreSQL, support **data compression** for both tables and indexes. By compressing large tables, you can reduce storage requirements and improve data retrieval times, as less data is being read from disk.

Here's an example of enabling row-level compression in SQL Server:

sql
Copy
```
ALTER TABLE large_table REBUILD PARTITION = ALL WITH
(DATA_COMPRESSION = PAGE);
```
By enabling compression, you can significantly reduce the disk space required for large tables and improve the overall performance of read-intensive queries.

9. Using Temporary Tables can also be helpful when working with large datasets, particularly for **intermediate results**. Instead of performing complex joins or aggregations repeatedly, you can store intermediate results in temporary tables. Temporary tables are stored in memory, making them faster to access than repeatedly querying large base tables.

For example:

sql
Copy
```
-- Create a temporary table to store intermediate results
CREATE TABLE #temp_results AS
SELECT product_id, SUM(sales_amount) AS total_sales
FROM sales
GROUP BY product_id;

-- Query from the temporary table
SELECT * FROM #temp_results WHERE total_sales > 10000;
```
Temporary tables can help improve performance by reducing the need to recompute complex operations or filter large datasets multiple times.

10. Distributed Databases are another strategy for handling large datasets, especially when the dataset is too large to fit on a single server. Distributed databases split data across multiple physical machines, allowing for parallel processing and load balancing. Technologies like **Sharding** (distributing data across multiple servers) or **Replication** (duplicating data across servers for high availability and performance) are commonly used in distributed systems.

If your database is growing rapidly, consider employing **distributed architectures** to scale your data across multiple servers. This approach allows you to handle more data without sacrificing performance by distributing the load.

11. In conclusion, managing **large datasets** in SQL requires a combination of best practices and optimization techniques. By leveraging **indexes**, **partitioning**, **batch processing**, and techniques like **compression** and **parallelism**, you can keep queries fast and responsive even as data volumes increase. Don't forget the importance of **data archiving** and **query optimization**, both of which can significantly reduce the load on your primary dataset and improve overall database performance.

12. In the next chapter, we'll explore **advanced database design principles**, where we'll cover strategies for building efficient and scalable databases from the ground up. This will include normalization, denormalization, and techniques for handling complex relationships within your data model. Get ready to take your database design skills to the next level! Happy querying and managing large datasets!

13. Another important consideration when dealing with **large datasets** is **query rewriting**. Sometimes, optimizing queries isn't just about indexing or adding hardware; it's about how you structure your SQL. Often, queries that seem simple can be inefficient because of their design. For instance, you may have a complex `JOIN` or a subquery that could be replaced with a more efficient approach.

Let's consider an example where a subquery is used inefficiently:

sql
Copy
```sql
-- Inefficient: Using a subquery to calculate the total
sales for each product
SELECT product_id,
       (SELECT SUM(sales_amount) FROM sales WHERE
product_id = p.product_id) AS total_sales
FROM products p;
```
This query is inefficient because for each product, it performs a subquery to sum the sales, which results in multiple queries being executed. Instead, you could use a `JOIN` and an aggregate function:

sql
Copy
```sql
-- More efficient: Using a JOIN with an aggregate function
SELECT p.product_id, SUM(s.sales_amount) AS total_sales
FROM products p
JOIN sales s ON p.product_id = s.product_id
GROUP BY p.product_id;
```

This rewritten query performs much better because it calculates the total sales in a single pass, reducing redundant operations and improving efficiency, especially when working with large datasets.

14. Dealing with Outliers in large datasets is another critical optimization strategy. When working with huge amounts of data, you may encounter **outliers**—data points that fall far outside the normal range. These outliers can affect the performance of aggregations, sorting, and indexing.

A good approach when working with outliers is to:

- **Identify and exclude outliers** if they don't contribute to the overall analysis.

- **Use approximate techniques** for large datasets (such as `APPROX_COUNT_DISTINCT()` in some database systems) to get results faster without fully processing the dataset.

- **Partition your data** to ensure that outliers are isolated and don't affect the general performance of your queries.

For example, if you're working with a `transactions` table and need to find average transaction amounts but suspect there are high-value outliers, you could exclude them:

```sql
Copy
SELECT AVG(transaction_amount)
FROM transactions
WHERE transaction_amount < 10000;
```
This query excludes transactions over a certain amount, which helps to ensure that the dataset you're analyzing is more representative and that outliers don't skew your performance metrics.

15. Load Balancing and **Replication** are two strategies that come into play when working with large datasets across distributed systems. If you're handling a large dataset that's too big for a single machine, load balancing and replication can distribute the query load across multiple servers to speed up performance. Replication can also provide high availability and fault tolerance by duplicating data across different systems.

For example, in **read-heavy applications**, you might use **read replicas** to distribute query load across multiple servers, ensuring that read requests don't overwhelm the primary database. With replication, your system can route read queries to replicas while maintaining write operations on the primary server:

```sql
Copy
-- Routing read queries to replicas
SELECT * FROM product_data; -- Query on read replica
```

In such cases, make sure to manage **synchronous replication** (for write consistency) and **asynchronous replication** (for higher read scalability) according to your system's needs.

16. Caching plays a vital role in optimizing queries on large datasets, particularly for frequently accessed data. **Query result caching** allows you to store the results of a query so that subsequent executions don't need to process the same data again, which can significantly reduce the load on your database.

Many modern databases have **built-in caching mechanisms**, but you can also implement **external caching** solutions like **Redis** or **Memcached** to store frequently requested data in-memory. For example, if a particular query to retrieve user details is frequently requested, you could cache the result and serve it from the cache rather than querying the database each time:

sql
Copy
```
-- Pseudocode for caching
cache.set('user_details_123', query_result)
```
This approach greatly reduces database load, especially for data that doesn't change frequently.

17. Query Parallelization is a technique that allows you to speed up the execution of large queries by splitting the query into multiple parts and running them in parallel. Many modern databases support parallel query execution, where queries are split into multiple tasks that can run on different CPU cores or even different servers.

For example, in **SQL Server**, you can set the MAXDOP (maximum degree of parallelism) hint to control the number of CPU cores used for query parallelization:

sql
Copy
```
SELECT * FROM large_table
OPTION (MAXDOP 4); -- Use up to 4 CPU cores for parallel
execution
```
By enabling parallel execution, you can significantly reduce query times on large datasets, especially for complex JOINs or aggregate queries.

18. Sharding is a technique often used in distributed databases to handle extremely large datasets. Sharding involves breaking a large table into smaller, more manageable pieces, or **shards**, each of which resides on a separate server or cluster. This enables the database to distribute the workload across multiple servers and reduces the burden on any single server.

For example, you might shard a customer table by **region** or by **customer_id range**. This ensures that data is evenly distributed, which prevents any one server from becoming a bottleneck. It's particularly useful when dealing with very high-traffic applications that need to scale horizontally.

19. Asynchronous Processing is another powerful strategy for managing large datasets. In some situations, running long-running queries or batch processes asynchronously can prevent them from blocking other operations. By allowing queries to run in the background, you can free up resources for other tasks and allow users to continue interacting with the database without delay.

For example, in a data warehouse environment, you may want to run ETL (Extract, Transform, Load) jobs asynchronously to aggregate and analyze data over time:

sql
Copy
```
-- Using job scheduling tools to run ETL jobs
asynchronously
EXECUTE Async_ETL_Process;
```
Asynchronous jobs can also be scheduled to run during off-peak hours, ensuring that heavy processes don't impact user experience during high-traffic times.

20. Batch Updates and Inserts are essential when dealing with large datasets, especially for **data migration** or when dealing with streaming data. Instead of inserting or updating records one by one, you can group them into batches to minimize the overhead of individual transactions. By processing records in batches, you can significantly improve the performance of these operations and reduce the load on the database.

For example, instead of running:

sql
Copy
```
INSERT INTO sales (product_id, quantity, price) VALUES (1,
100, 29.99);
INSERT INTO sales (product_id, quantity, price) VALUES (2,
200, 19.99);
```
You could use:

sql
Copy
```
INSERT INTO sales (product_id, quantity, price)
VALUES
(1, 100, 29.99),
(2, 200, 19.99);
```
This reduces the overhead of committing each insert and improves overall insert speed.

21. In conclusion, handling **large datasets** in SQL requires a blend of smart query design, proper database architecture, and careful resource management. By using **indexing**, **partitioning**, **batch processing**, **parallelization**, and **caching**, you can significantly improve query performance and ensure that your SQL queries remain fast and efficient. Additionally, techniques like **sharding**

and **asynchronous processing** allow you to scale your database effectively and handle massive amounts of data without overwhelming your system.

22. In the next chapter, we will explore **advanced database design principles**, where we will delve into key strategies for creating databases that are both scalable and efficient. Topics such as **normalization**, **denormalization**, and handling **complex relationships** will be covered to help you structure your database to better manage and scale large datasets. Database design plays a crucial role in ensuring that your system can handle high volumes of data while maintaining performance. We'll also look at best practices for designing tables, creating indexes, and ensuring data integrity, all while optimizing for performance.

By understanding the foundational principles of database design, you'll be able to create systems that are both responsive and robust, no matter how much data you're dealing with. Get ready to dive into the next level of database architecture as we continue our exploration of advanced SQL concepts!

23. Before we wrap up, remember that managing large datasets is a continuous process. It's not just about writing efficient queries, but also about **proactively monitoring** and **maintaining** the health of your database. Regularly check for performance bottlenecks, re-evaluate your indexing strategy, and optimize queries as your dataset evolves. Additionally, as your data grows, consider using distributed systems, cloud-based solutions, and other cutting-edge technologies that help ensure your database can handle increasing loads.

In real-world applications, performance tuning and optimization aren't one-time fixes—they require **ongoing attention** and adjustments based on changes in data, user behavior, and query patterns. By staying ahead of potential issues and adopting best practices, you can ensure your database remains efficient, responsive, and scalable.

24. That's it for Chapter 20! Working with large datasets can be daunting, but with the right strategies, tools, and mindset, you'll be able to manage and query big data effectively. From partitioning and indexing to batch processing and parallelism, there's a wide range of techniques you can use to optimize SQL queries and keep your system performing at its best. As you move forward, keep experimenting with these techniques, monitor their impact on your queries, and refine your approach to match your specific data requirements.

25. In the next chapter, we'll dive deeper into **advanced database design principles**, and you'll learn how to design and architect databases that can scale efficiently with large amounts of data while maintaining high performance. You'll also gain insights into how normalization and denormalization play crucial roles in optimizing your database design. Let's continue building on the foundation of database management and optimization skills you've developed so far. Happy designing, and get ready for more advanced concepts in the world of SQL!

Chapter 21: Full-Text Search and Advanced Filtering

1. Welcome to Chapter 21! In this chapter, we'll explore **Full-Text Search** and **Advanced Filtering** techniques—two powerful tools that allow you to work with text-based data efficiently. Whether you're working with large datasets that include textual information or need to implement sophisticated search capabilities, full-text search and advanced filtering are key to handling complex queries. These techniques allow for fast, accurate, and flexible text-based searching, something traditional SQL queries often struggle with when handling large volumes of unstructured data. By the end of this chapter, you'll have a strong understanding of how to use these tools to enhance your querying capabilities.

2. Let's start by defining **Full-Text Search**. Full-text search is a specialized search technique that allows you to search for words or phrases within textual data quickly and efficiently. Unlike traditional SQL queries that rely on simple `LIKE` operators, full-text search is designed to handle large amounts of text, indexing the words in columns so that searches can be performed much faster. This is particularly useful when you have a table with large text fields such as product descriptions, customer reviews, or blog posts.

For example, if you have a `products` table with a `description` column, full-text search can be used to quickly find products that contain specific words or phrases within the description.

3. To implement **Full-Text Search** in SQL, you typically need to create a **full-text index** on the column that contains the textual data you want to search. Here's an example using SQL Server:

```sql
Copy
CREATE FULLTEXT INDEX ON products(description)
KEY INDEX pk_products;
```

This command creates a full-text index on the `description` column of the `products` table. The index allows the database to store a catalog of the words in that column, which speeds up search queries significantly compared to traditional methods.

4. Once the full-text index is created, you can use the `CONTAINS` or `FREETEXT` predicates in your queries to search the indexed text:

```sql
Copy
SELECT product_id, product_name
FROM products
WHERE CONTAINS(description, 'organic');
```

This query finds all products whose descriptions contain the word "organic." The `CONTAINS` predicate is much faster and more flexible than using `LIKE '%organic%'`, especially when searching through large volumes of text.

5. Full-text search also supports **advanced features** like searching for phrases, proximity searches, and wildcard searches. For example, you can search for a **phrase** by enclosing the words in double quotes:

```sql
Copy
```

```sql
SELECT product_id, product_name
FROM products
WHERE CONTAINS(description, '"natural ingredients"');
```
This query will only return products whose descriptions contain the exact phrase "natural ingredients." You can also search for words **near** each other with proximity search:

```sql
sql
Copy
SELECT product_id, product_name
FROM products
WHERE CONTAINS(description, '"natural" NEAR
"ingredients"');
```
This will return results where the words "natural" and "ingredients" appear close to each other, but not necessarily in the exact order.

6. Wildcards can also be used in full-text searches to match variations of a word. For example, you can search for all words that start with "bio" by using an asterisk (*):

```sql
sql
Copy
SELECT product_id, product_name
FROM products
WHERE CONTAINS(description, 'bio*');
```
This query will match words like "bio," "biodegradable," "biodiversity," and more. Wildcards are incredibly useful for broadening your search scope when you need to capture variations of a root word.

7. Advanced Filtering is another crucial topic when working with large datasets, especially when you need to refine the results returned by your queries. SQL provides a variety of filtering techniques that can help you drill down into your data and retrieve only the information you need. The most common way to filter results is by using the WHERE clause with logical operators such as AND, OR, and NOT.

For example, if you want to find all products with a price greater than $50 and that contain the word "organic" in the description, you can combine filters:

```sql
sql
Copy
SELECT product_id, product_name, price
FROM products
WHERE price > 50 AND CONTAINS(description, 'organic');
```
By combining filters, you can narrow down your search results to match multiple criteria, improving the accuracy and relevance of the data you retrieve.

8. Another powerful filtering feature is **range filtering**, which allows you to find records within a specific range of values. You can filter on numerical, date, or even textual data ranges. For example, to find products added in the last 30 days, you can use a range filter with a date column:

```sql
Copy
SELECT product_id, product_name, added_date
FROM products
WHERE added_date BETWEEN '2025-03-01' AND '2025-03-31';
```
This will return products added during March 2025. Range filtering is particularly useful when working with time-sensitive data, like sales or inventory updates.

9. Null Values can often be overlooked but are an important aspect of filtering. When dealing with datasets that may contain missing or unknown data, SQL provides the IS NULL or IS NOT NULL operators to check for NULL values. For instance, if you want to find products that have no description, you can write:

```sql
Copy
SELECT product_id, product_name
FROM products
WHERE description IS NULL;
```
This query will return all products that lack a description. Similarly, you can filter for records where a value is not NULL by using IS NOT NULL.

10. Pattern Matching is another advanced filtering technique, and it is particularly useful for working with text data. The LIKE operator is commonly used for pattern matching, allowing you to search for text that matches a specific pattern. For example, to find products whose names start with "eco," you can use the LIKE operator:

```sql
Copy
SELECT product_id, product_name
FROM products
WHERE product_name LIKE 'eco%';
```
This will return all products that have names starting with "eco." The percent sign (%) acts as a wildcard to match any characters following "eco". Similarly, you can use the underscore (_) wildcard to match a single character.

11. Combining Full-Text Search and Advanced Filtering is often necessary when you need to filter text data with multiple conditions. By combining the power of full-text search with standard filtering techniques, you can build highly efficient, complex queries. For instance, to find products containing "organic" in the description, priced over $50, and available in stock, you could write:

```sql
Copy
SELECT product_id, product_name, price
FROM products
WHERE CONTAINS(description, 'organic')
AND price > 50
AND stock_quantity > 0;
```

This approach ensures that you only return products that meet all your search and filtering criteria, making your queries both efficient and precise. By combining text search with numeric or categorical filters (like `price` and `stock_quantity`), you can create a query that's both fast and accurate, providing your users with exactly the data they need.

12. Nested Filters allow you to refine your results even further by applying multiple layers of filtering. For example, you could apply full-text search first to narrow down the dataset, and then use more specific filters for sorting or selecting a subset of the data. Here's an example of using a **nested filter** approach to find the most relevant products, sorted by price, and only considering those within a specific price range:

```sql
Copy
SELECT product_id, product_name, price
FROM products
WHERE CONTAINS(description, 'organic')
AND price BETWEEN 20 AND 100
ORDER BY price DESC;
```

This query first uses full-text search to find products containing the word "organic" in their description. Then, it filters out products that don't meet the price range condition and orders the results by price. This technique is particularly useful when you need a refined subset of data that matches several specific conditions, including text search.

13. Case-Insensitive Searches are another advanced filtering consideration, especially when working with case-sensitive databases. In many databases, searches using `LIKE` or even `CONTAINS` can be case-sensitive depending on the database's collation settings. This can result in unexpected results if users search for terms in different cases (e.g., "Organic" vs. "organic").

To perform a **case-insensitive search** in SQL, you can use the `LOWER()` or `UPPER()` function to normalize the case of both the search term and the column being searched. For example:

```sql
Copy
```

```sql
SELECT product_id, product_name
FROM products
WHERE LOWER(description) LIKE '%organic%';
```
By using **LOWER()** on both the column and the search term, this query ensures that the search is case-insensitive, matching "organic," "Organic," or "ORGANIC" without issues.

14. Range Queries with Multiple Conditions can be particularly helpful when working with large datasets that contain data with a range of values, such as dates, prices, or ratings. These types of queries often combine full-text search with range filtering to narrow down results. For example, suppose you want to find books that are tagged with "science" in their descriptions and were published in the last 10 years, with prices between $20 and $100:

sql
Copy
```sql
SELECT book_id, title, price, publish_date
FROM books
WHERE CONTAINS(description, 'science')
AND publish_date BETWEEN '2013-01-01' AND '2023-01-01'
AND price BETWEEN 20 AND 100
ORDER BY publish_date DESC;
```
This query combines full-text search for the keyword "science" with multiple filters for publication date and price range. The combination of these filters ensures that the results are both relevant and within the user's specified constraints.

15. Handling Large Datasets with Full-Text Search requires careful consideration of system performance. While full-text search can be much faster than traditional **LIKE** searches, indexing large text fields in databases with billions of rows can still be resource-intensive. You need to be mindful of how often the full-text index needs to be updated (especially in systems where data is constantly changing) and how that affects database performance.

In high-volume environments, consider using a dedicated **search engine** like **Elasticsearch** or **Apache Solr**, which are optimized for full-text search and are designed to scale to handle large datasets efficiently. These external tools allow you to index and search data in a way that's much more efficient than relying solely on traditional relational database systems.

16. Full-Text Search Performance Tuning is another crucial aspect to consider. One approach is to ensure that full-text indexes are **up-to-date** and optimized for the types of queries you are running. You can periodically rebuild the index to ensure it's performing as efficiently as possible:

sql
Copy
```sql
ALTER FULLTEXT INDEX ON products REBUILD;
```

Additionally, be sure to monitor the performance of your full-text search queries using execution plans. Look for costly operations such as table scans or inefficient index usage, and use the query optimizer to adjust indexing strategies.

Another optimization technique is to reduce the frequency of complex full-text searches by caching results. If you frequently search for the same terms, caching those results can save valuable processing time and database resources.

17. Ranking and Relevance in Full-Text Search is a powerful way to prioritize search results based on their relevance to the search term. Most full-text search systems, including SQL Server, provide built-in functions that allow you to rank search results based on how closely they match the query.

In SQL Server, you can use the RANK() function or CONTAINS with FREETEXT to determine the relevance of search results:

sql
Copy
```sql
SELECT product_id, product_name, price,
       RANK() OVER (ORDER BY FREETEXT(description, 'organic')) AS relevance
FROM products
WHERE CONTAINS(description, 'organic')
ORDER BY relevance DESC;
```
This query ranks products based on how well their descriptions match the term "organic," returning the most relevant products at the top of the list. Ranking can significantly improve the user experience in applications with large datasets, as it ensures that the most relevant results are presented first.

18. Faceted Search is another advanced technique that enhances filtering by allowing users to filter by multiple categories or facets, such as price range, brand, or color, while also performing full-text searches. For example, a user searching for "organic" products might want to filter results by price or category as well.

In SQL, this type of filtering can be achieved by using multiple WHERE clauses or AND conditions combined with the full-text search:

sql
Copy
```sql
SELECT product_id, product_name, category, price
FROM products
WHERE CONTAINS(description, 'organic')
AND price BETWEEN 10 AND 50
AND category = 'Health';
```

This allows for sophisticated filtering, making it easier for users to narrow down results and find exactly what they're looking for. This approach is commonly used in e-commerce platforms, product catalogs, and other applications where multiple facets of data need to be considered simultaneously.

19. Considerations for Internationalization in full-text search are important when working with multilingual datasets. Full-text search systems can be customized to handle different languages by using language-specific tokenizers and stemming algorithms. For example, in SQL Server, you can create full-text indexes that support multiple languages, such as English, French, or Spanish, ensuring that your searches work across different languages and characters sets:

sql
Copy
```
CREATE FULLTEXT INDEX ON products(description)
LANGUAGE 1033;  -- 1033 is the language ID for English
```
This ensures that the database can search more accurately for words in different languages, taking into account language-specific rules for word stemming and inflection.

20. In conclusion, **Full-Text Search** and **Advanced Filtering** are invaluable tools for working with text-heavy data in SQL. Full-text search enables you to perform fast, efficient text searches on large datasets, while advanced filtering techniques allow you to refine and narrow your results based on specific criteria. By combining full-text search with filtering, ranking, and faceted search, you can deliver high-performance, flexible search functionality in your applications.

21. In the next chapter, we will delve into **Advanced Data Types and Functions**, which will allow you to handle more complex data structures, such as JSON, XML, and spatial data. These data types require specialized functions and queries to work with them effectively, offering you a powerful way to manage and analyze non-tabular data within your SQL database. As SQL continues to evolve, it's becoming increasingly important to be able to work with these advanced data types to keep up with modern data needs.

For instance, JSON has become the standard for many applications due to its flexibility and human-readable format. XML is still widely used for document storage, especially for integration with web services. Spatial data, such as geolocation information, is crucial for applications dealing with maps and locations. By mastering the techniques for querying and manipulating these advanced data types, you'll be able to handle a broad spectrum of data in your databases.

In this upcoming chapter, we'll explore how to store, query, and manipulate JSON, XML, and spatial data in SQL, using built-in SQL functions and tools specific to your DBMS. With the rise of semi-structured data formats and the increasing importance of location-based services, these skills will make you a more effective SQL developer. So, get ready to expand your SQL toolkit and dive into the world of advanced data types!

Happy searching, filtering, and preparing to take your SQL knowledge even further!

Chapter 22: Data Backup, Recovery, and High Availability

1. Welcome to Chapter 22! In this chapter, we will dive into some of the most critical aspects of database management—**Data Backup**, **Recovery**, and **High Availability**. As your databases grow and become central to the operation of your applications, ensuring that your data is safe and can be quickly restored in case of failure is vital. Similarly, high availability ensures that your database remains accessible and responsive, even during hardware failures, network issues, or other interruptions. By the end of this chapter, you'll have a solid understanding of how to protect your data and maintain your database systems' availability, ensuring minimal downtime and data loss.

2. Let's start with the basics of **Data Backup**. A **backup** is a copy of your data that is stored separately from the primary database, ensuring that you can restore it in case of data corruption, hardware failure, or accidental deletion. Backups are an essential part of any data management strategy and can be classified into three primary types: **full backups**, **differential backups**, and **transaction log backups**.

- **Full Backups**: This is a complete copy of the entire database, including all tables, indexes, and objects. Full backups are the most comprehensive, but they can be large and time-consuming to create.

- **Differential Backups**: These backups capture all changes made since the last full backup. They are faster to create than full backups but are still relatively comprehensive.

- **Transaction Log Backups**: These backups capture all transaction logs generated since the last backup, allowing you to restore the database to a specific point in time. Transaction log backups are particularly useful for point-in-time recovery.

A typical backup strategy will use a combination of these backup types, with periodic full backups, more frequent differential backups, and regular transaction log backups.

3. When planning your **backup strategy**, it's essential to understand the **backup window**—the period in which backups can be safely taken without impacting normal database operations. The backup window will depend on several factors, including the size of your database, the frequency of changes, and your system's resources. For large databases, it may not be feasible to perform full backups during peak hours due to the impact on performance. In such cases, you can schedule backups during off-peak hours and rely on **differential backups** or **transaction log backups** during the day to keep the backup process efficient and manageable.

For example, you might set up the following strategy:

- Perform a **full backup** every Sunday at 2 AM when traffic is low.

- Perform **differential backups** every 12 hours (e.g., 2 PM and 2 AM) on weekdays.

- Perform **transaction log backups** every 15 minutes throughout the day to minimize data loss in the event of a failure.

This strategy ensures you maintain regular backups without overloading the system during peak usage times.

4. One of the most critical aspects of any backup and recovery plan is **testing your backups**. It's not enough to just create backups; you must regularly verify that you can restore them successfully. Failure to test backups can lead to nasty surprises when you need to perform a recovery. Regularly test your backup process by restoring backups in a controlled environment to ensure they're working as expected.

For example, you can set up a test server and periodically restore a full backup to verify that the data can be successfully recovered:

sql
Copy
```sql
-- Restoring a full backup to a test database
RESTORE DATABASE your_test_database
FROM DISK = 'C:\backups\your_database.bak'
WITH REPLACE;
```
Testing your backups ensures that the recovery process will be smooth when the time comes, and it helps identify potential issues with the backup process that need to be addressed before an actual disaster occurs.

5. Point-in-Time Recovery allows you to restore a database to a specific moment in time, which is especially useful when dealing with data corruption, human errors, or malicious activities. This type of recovery is only possible when you have **transaction log backups** in place, as they capture all the changes made to the database since the last full or differential backup.

For example, if a user accidentally deleted important data at 10:15 AM, and you have transaction log backups taken every 15 minutes, you can restore the database from the last full backup (let's say 9 AM) and then apply the transaction log backups up until just before 10:15 AM, effectively rolling the database back to its state before the deletion occurred.

sql
Copy
```sql
-- Restoring a full backup
RESTORE DATABASE your_database
FROM DISK = 'C:\backups\your_database.bak'
WITH NORECOVERY;

-- Applying transaction log backups
RESTORE LOG your_database
FROM DISK = 'C:\backups\your_database_log.trn'
WITH STOPAT = '2025-04-09 10:14:00', NORECOVERY;
```
The WITH STOPAT option allows you to specify the exact time you want to restore the database to, giving you fine-grained control over your recovery process.

6. High Availability (HA) setups are designed to ensure that your database remains available even in the event of hardware failures, network issues, or other unexpected disruptions. In an HA setup, multiple copies of your database (known as **replicas**) are maintained, with automatic failover mechanisms in place to minimize downtime.

There are several ways to achieve high availability in SQL databases, depending on the system you're using. For instance, **SQL Server** offers several high-availability solutions, such as **Always On Availability Groups** and **Database Mirroring**, while **MySQL** provides **Master-Slave Replication** and **Group Replication**.

In **SQL Server**, **Always On Availability Groups** allow you to configure multiple replicas of a database, with one primary replica that handles read and write operations, and secondary replicas that maintain real-time copies of the data. If the primary replica becomes unavailable, one of the secondary replicas can automatically take over with minimal downtime.

For example, setting up an Always On Availability Group typically involves:

- Configuring a **Windows Server Failover Cluster (WSFC)**.

- Enabling Always On Availability Groups on SQL Server.

- Creating and configuring the availability group, which includes defining the primary and secondary replicas.

7. Failover Clustering is another important high-availability technique, particularly for environments that require uninterrupted database service. In a failover cluster, two or more servers are linked together, sharing storage and resources. If one server fails, another server in the cluster automatically takes over, minimizing downtime. This approach is often used in critical systems that cannot afford extended periods of unavailability.

For example, in **SQL Server**, you can create a **Windows Server Failover Cluster** (WSFC) to implement a failover solution. The cluster ensures that the database service can continue running on a different node (server) in the event of a failure, ensuring high availability.

Here's a simplified example of setting up failover:

- Install SQL Server on multiple nodes.

- Configure shared storage (SAN or SMB file share).

- Set up the cluster using the **Failover Cluster Manager** in Windows Server.

- Add SQL Server instances to the cluster.

8. Replication is a high-availability technique that involves copying and distributing data from one database (the **master**) to one or more other databases (the **slaves**). Replication is commonly used in read-heavy environments, where multiple replicas can handle read queries, while the master handles writes.

There are different types of replication:

- **Master-Slave Replication**: One master database handles writes, while one or more slave databases replicate the data from the master and handle read queries.

- **Peer-to-Peer Replication**: Each node in the replication topology is both a master and a replica, allowing both read and write operations on all nodes.

- **Multi-Master Replication**: Multiple databases can accept write operations, and changes are propagated across all nodes.

In **MySQL**, setting up **Master-Slave Replication** involves configuring the master to log changes and then configuring the slave(s) to read those logs and replicate the data.

9. Cloud-Based High Availability is becoming increasingly popular due to its flexibility and scalability. Cloud providers like **Amazon Web Services (AWS)**, **Microsoft Azure**, and **Google Cloud** offer managed database services with built-in high availability features. For example, **Amazon RDS** (Relational Database Service) offers automatic backups, multi-AZ (Availability Zone) replication, and automatic failover without requiring you to manage your own infrastructure.

In **Azure SQL Database**, high availability is achieved through **Geo-Replication** and **Zone-Redundant Deployments**, which replicate your database across multiple regions or availability zones. These services ensure that your data is resilient to regional failures and can failover automatically if needed.

For example, in AWS, setting up **Multi-AZ** deployments in RDS automatically synchronizes your primary database with a secondary replica in another availability zone. In case of a failure, RDS automatically switches to the secondary replica, ensuring minimal downtime.

10. Monitoring High Availability: Whether you are using replication, failover clustering, or a cloud service, it's essential to monitor the health and performance of your high-availability setup. Monitoring ensures that any issues are detected early, before they impact your database's availability.

You should set up automated monitoring for key performance indicators (KPIs) such as:

- **Replica synchronization**: Ensure that replicas are up-to-date with the primary database.

- **Failover readiness**: Check the health of the failover mechanism and whether it's able to take over in the event of a failure.

- **Performance metrics**: Monitor query performance and latency, especially in replicated or clustered environments.

You can use tools like **SQL Server Management Studio (SSMS)**, **AWS CloudWatch**, or **Azure Monitor** to track and set up alerts for any issues in your high-availability configuration.

11. In conclusion, **data backup**, **recovery**, and **high availability** are crucial components of any robust database strategy. Regular, tested backups, point-in-time recovery, and high-availability setups such as replication and failover clusters ensure that your data is protected, recoverable, and always available to users, even in the event of a failure. Implementing these practices is essential for maintaining the reliability and uptime of your critical databases.

12. In the next chapter, we'll explore **advanced security features** in SQL, covering topics like encryption, user roles, permissions, and securing access to your database. As your database infrastructure grows, ensuring the security of your data becomes even more important. Let's continue building secure, scalable, and reliable systems together! Happy backing up, recovering, and ensuring your databases are always available!

13. One of the most important aspects of maintaining a high-availability environment is **automating** your backup and recovery processes. Automation ensures that you don't miss backups or have to manually intervene during a failure. Most modern database management systems (DBMS) have built-in automation features for backups, restores, and failovers. For example, in **SQL Server**, you can use **SQL Server Agent** to schedule regular backups, run recovery jobs, and even monitor the health of your high-availability system.

Here's an example of setting up an automated backup job:

```sql
Copy
USE msdb;
GO
EXEC sp_add_job
    @job_name = 'Database Backup Job';
GO
EXEC sp_add_jobstep
    @job_name = 'Database Backup Job',
    @step_name = 'Full Backup',
    @subsystem = 'TSQL',
    @command = 'BACKUP DATABASE your_database TO DISK =
''C:\backups\your_database.bak''',
    @database_name = 'master';
GO
EXEC sp_add_schedule
    @schedule_name = 'Daily Backup',
    @freq_type = 4, -- Daily
    @freq_interval = 1, -- Every day
    @active_start_time = 020000; -- 2 AM
GO
EXEC sp_attach_schedule
```

```sql
    @job_name = 'Database Backup Job',
    @schedule_name = 'Daily Backup';
GO
```
This script automates the backup process, running it every day at 2 AM. By automating these tasks, you can ensure that backups are performed regularly without human error and that your recovery systems are always up-to-date.

14. Another valuable practice is to **store backups off-site** or use **cloud storage** solutions for your backup files. Storing backups on-site (e.g., on the same physical hardware as your database) leaves your data vulnerable to hardware failures, disasters, or even theft. Cloud backup solutions such as **Amazon S3**, **Azure Blob Storage**, or **Google Cloud Storage** offer secure, scalable, and cost-effective ways to store backups off-site, ensuring that your data remains safe even if the primary database server fails.

Cloud-based backups also integrate seamlessly with high-availability configurations. For instance, in **Amazon RDS**, you can enable automated backups, which are stored in Amazon S3 and can be used for quick recovery or point-in-time restoration.

15. Data Retention Policies are another essential element of your backup and recovery strategy. While it's important to keep regular backups, it's also crucial to manage **how long** backups are kept. Storing backups indefinitely can quickly lead to massive storage consumption, especially in large-scale environments. A good retention policy specifies how long to keep each type of backup—typically, full backups may be kept for a few weeks or months, differential backups for a shorter period, and transaction logs for the shortest time (e.g., a few days or a week).

Here's an example of implementing a basic backup retention policy:

- Keep **full backups** for 30 days.

- Keep **differential backups** for 7 days.

- Keep **transaction log backups** for 2 days.

By regularly **pruning old backups**, you ensure that your backup system remains efficient and manageable without consuming excessive storage resources.

16. Testing Failover Mechanisms is a critical part of your high-availability strategy. A failover mechanism ensures that, if one part of your system goes down, another part takes over without affecting users. It's not enough to configure failover once and forget about it; you must **test failover processes** regularly to ensure that they work as expected during a failure scenario.

In **SQL Server Always On Availability Groups**, for example, you can simulate a failover by manually switching the primary replica to one of the secondary replicas to verify that it becomes the new primary. Here's a basic example of how to force a manual failover:

sql
Copy

```
ALTER AVAILABILITY GROUP your_availability_group
FORCE_FAILOVER_ALLOW_DATA_LOSS;
```
Testing failover ensures that your high-availability setup will work smoothly when it's needed most, giving you confidence that your database will remain operational, even during unexpected outages.

17. Disaster Recovery Drills should be conducted regularly to ensure your team is prepared for worst-case scenarios. A disaster recovery drill involves simulating a disaster—such as hardware failure, database corruption, or a complete data center outage—and then following the recovery procedures to bring the database back online. These drills help identify gaps in your disaster recovery plan and allow your team to practice the recovery process.

For example, if you're using a multi-region **cloud-based system** like **Azure SQL Database** or **Amazon RDS**, you can simulate a failover to another region and test how quickly your system can recover. This practice can also help determine how long the failover will take and whether any manual intervention is required.

18. High Availability Monitoring is essential for ensuring the smooth operation of your system. Without proper monitoring, it's difficult to detect issues that could lead to system downtime or degraded performance. In a high-availability setup, you need to monitor the health of the replicas, the synchronization of data, and the overall system performance. You should also set up automated alerts for events like replica lag, failover status, or server failures.

For example, in **SQL Server**, you can use **SQL Server Management Studio (SSMS)** to monitor Always On Availability Groups. The **Dashboard** provides a real-time view of your replicas' health, allowing you to quickly detect and respond to issues:

sql
Copy
```
SELECT * FROM sys.dm_hadr_availability_group_states;
```
This query provides information about the status of the availability group, such as whether the replica is healthy and whether it's the primary or secondary replica.

19. Cloud Services and Managed Databases offer a great deal of convenience when it comes to backup, recovery, and high availability. Services like **Amazon RDS**, **Azure SQL Database**, and **Google Cloud SQL** provide built-in features like automated backups, multi-region replication, and high-availability configurations. These cloud-based services handle much of the heavy lifting for you, offering automatic backup scheduling, failover, and replication across multiple availability zones or regions.

While using these services greatly simplifies the process of implementing a high-availability and recovery strategy, it's still important to understand the underlying mechanisms. You'll need to be familiar with the tools provided by the cloud provider for managing backups, monitoring health, and performing restores.

20. In conclusion, **Data Backup**, **Recovery**, and **High Availability** are essential practices that every database administrator must master. With a solid backup strategy in place, you can rest assured that your data is safe and can be recovered in the event of a failure. High-availability solutions such as replication, failover clustering, and cloud-based services ensure that your database remains available to users at all times, even during hardware failures or other disruptions. Testing your backups, recovery procedures, and failover mechanisms is crucial to ensuring that your system will perform as expected when needed most.

21. As we've seen throughout this chapter, **Data Backup**, **Recovery**, and **High Availability** are cornerstones of a robust and resilient database infrastructure. Implementing a solid backup strategy with full, differential, and transaction log backups ensures that you can recover data in the event of a disaster, while point-in-time recovery gives you granular control over how and when to restore your database. Furthermore, high availability ensures that your database can remain operational even when hardware failures or other disruptions occur, minimizing downtime and improving user experience.

To maximize the effectiveness of your data management strategy, make sure to combine these techniques with **monitoring**, **testing**, and **automation**. Regularly monitor your backup processes, replicate data to remote or cloud-based servers for added safety, and test your recovery mechanisms frequently. This proactive approach will help you identify and address potential issues before they affect your operations.

Additionally, whether you're using **on-premise** solutions like SQL Server's Always On Availability Groups or **cloud-based services** like Amazon RDS or Azure SQL, understanding the underlying principles of these high-availability setups will ensure that you can efficiently manage and optimize them.

As databases continue to grow in size and complexity, these strategies will become even more crucial to your ability to keep data safe, recoverable, and highly available. Investing in reliable backup and recovery procedures will provide peace of mind and ensure that your system can handle unexpected failures without causing major disruptions.

22. In the next chapter, we'll explore **Advanced Security Features** in SQL, such as encryption, user roles, and permissions management. As your database grows, so does the need to protect it from unauthorized access and ensure sensitive information is safeguarded. We'll look at the best practices for securing your SQL database, managing users and roles, and implementing encryption both for data-at-rest and data-in-transit. Understanding how to secure your database infrastructure is as crucial as managing backups and availability.

Let's continue building secure, scalable, and reliable database systems together! Happy securing, and let's dive into advanced security practices next!

Chapter 23: SQL Server Management Tools and GUI Interfaces

1. Welcome to Chapter 23! In this chapter, we will explore the powerful **SQL Server Management Tools** and **GUI interfaces** that help database administrators and developers work more efficiently with SQL Server. Whether you're managing a small database or working with a large-scale enterprise solution, the right tools can make database management, querying, and troubleshooting faster and easier. By the end of this chapter, you'll have a solid understanding of the various tools available to you and how to leverage them to streamline your work and enhance productivity.

2. Let's begin with **SQL Server Management Studio (SSMS)**, one of the most widely used tools for managing SQL Server. **SSMS** is an integrated environment that provides a graphical interface for database management, query execution, and administrative tasks. It is an essential tool for database professionals working with SQL Server, as it allows for easy access to SQL Server instances, enables query execution, and provides comprehensive features for database design, security management, and performance monitoring.

With SSMS, you can:

- **Connect to and manage SQL Server instances**.

- **Execute queries** with the built-in query editor.

- **Monitor and manage server activity**.

- **Configure security**, including user roles and permissions.

- **Create and manage database objects** like tables, views, stored procedures, and indexes.

Here's a quick look at how to connect to a SQL Server instance using SSMS:

1. Open SSMS and in the "Connect to Server" dialog, enter the **server name** and **authentication details**.

2. Once connected, you can use the **Object Explorer** to browse databases, tables, views, and other objects on the server.

3. SSMS also provides a **query editor** that supports features like syntax highlighting, code completion, and error detection. These features help you write and debug SQL queries more efficiently. For example, when writing a `SELECT` query, SSMS will suggest column names and table names based on what you type, reducing the chance of syntax errors and speeding up query writing.

In addition to the query editor, SSMS offers the ability to save and organize your queries in **SQL query windows** and **query files**. This allows you to work on multiple queries simultaneously without losing your work.

4. Another useful feature of SSMS is its **execution plan** functionality. The **execution plan** shows you how SQL Server is executing your queries, which can help you identify potential performance bottlenecks. In the query editor, you can easily generate an execution plan by clicking on the **Include Actual Execution Plan** button before running your query.

The execution plan breaks down the operations SQL Server is performing (such as index scans, joins, and sorts) and shows you their relative costs. This allows you to see where optimizations are needed and make informed decisions about indexing, query structure, or hardware resources.

5. SQL Server Profiler is another powerful tool included with SSMS that helps with performance monitoring and troubleshooting. It allows you to capture and analyze SQL Server events in real-time. You can track everything from user queries to internal server activities and analyze this data to identify issues such as slow queries, deadlocks, or resource-intensive operations.

SQL Server Profiler can be used to:

- **Monitor queries** being executed on the server.

- **Capture performance data** for troubleshooting.

- **Track database activities** like connections, logins, and transactions.

By filtering events and setting thresholds, you can focus on specific actions or processes that need attention. For instance, you might filter by query execution time to identify slow queries that need optimization.

6. SQL Server Data Tools (SSDT) is a set of tools within SSMS that allows for database development and design within Visual Studio. SSDT is designed for creating, testing, and deploying SQL Server databases in a **development environment**. With SSDT, you can:

- **Design and develop databases**.

- **Create database schemas** (tables, views, stored procedures).

- **Perform schema comparison** between different database versions.

- **Deploy** databases to different environments (test, staging, production).

SSDT provides a more integrated development experience, allowing you to work directly with SQL scripts, T-SQL code, and database objects within the Visual Studio IDE. If you're building complex database projects that involve code deployment and version control, SSDT is an invaluable tool.

7. For those who prefer a **web-based interface**, **SQL Server Management Studio Express (SSMSE)** offers a lightweight, simplified version of SSMS. SSMSE is designed for smaller databases or situations where you don't need the full functionality of SSMS. It provides a streamlined interface for managing SQL Server instances, executing queries, and performing basic administrative tasks.

However, SSMSE does have limitations, such as the absence of advanced features like **Profiler** or **Advanced Query Execution Plans**, making it better suited for simpler environments or lightweight database management tasks.

8. Azure Data Studio is another modern, cross-platform tool for managing SQL Server instances, and it's especially useful for those who need to work across multiple platforms (Windows, macOS, and Linux). Azure Data Studio has a clean, user-friendly interface with built-in features like:

- **Code snippets** to help write queries faster.

- **Integrated source control** (via Git).

- **Support for extensions** to add new features.

Azure Data Studio is an excellent alternative to SSMS for cloud-based SQL Server management, especially for users working in cloud environments like **Azure SQL Database**. It also supports **notebooks**, which allow you to combine code, results, and visualizations in a single interface—ideal for data scientists or analysts working with SQL and Python or R code.

9. SQLCMD is a command-line tool that allows you to run T-SQL commands and scripts directly from the command line, making it ideal for automation or when working in environments where a GUI is not available. SQLCMD is especially useful for automating SQL Server tasks and running scripts on multiple servers without needing a full GUI interface.

You can run SQLCMD from the command line like this:

```bash
sqlcmd -S server_name -d database_name -U user_name -P password -Q "SELECT * FROM your_table"
```

SQLCMD is a great tool for batch processing, job automation, or when working on remote servers without direct access to the graphical interface.

10. PowerShell is an essential tool for SQL Server administrators and developers, especially when working in automated environments or managing multiple servers. SQL Server provides a set of **PowerShell cmdlets** that allow you to manage databases, run queries, and automate tasks.

For example, you can use PowerShell to back up a database:

```powershell
Backup-SqlDatabase -ServerInstance "your_server" -Database "your_database" -BackupFile "C:\backups\your_database.bak"
```

PowerShell is highly customizable, allowing for scripting and automation of SQL Server tasks, making it an invaluable tool for database administrators who need to manage large or complex environments.

11. Third-Party Tools also play a significant role in SQL Server management, offering advanced features or simplified workflows that are not always present in the default management tools. Some popular third-party tools for SQL Server include:

- **Redgate SQL Toolbelt**: A suite of tools that simplifies database development, deployment, and management. It includes tools for database versioning, deployment automation, and query optimization.

- **ApexSQL**: Offers a range of SQL Server tools for database development, backup and recovery, and database auditing.

- **dbForge Studio**: A comprehensive IDE for SQL Server that provides advanced query editing, schema comparison, and reporting features.

These tools can be extremely helpful for specialized tasks such as version control, database deployment automation, and optimization. Depending on your needs, they can complement or extend the capabilities of SSMS and other SQL Server tools.

12. In conclusion, having the right **SQL Server Management Tools** and **GUI interfaces** is crucial for efficiently managing and optimizing your databases. Whether you're using the comprehensive features of **SQL Server Management Studio (SSMS)**, the lightweight version of **SQLCMD**, or the cross-platform flexibility of **Azure Data Studio**, each tool has its strengths. By understanding when and how to use these tools, you can streamline your workflow, improve productivity, and enhance the overall management of your SQL Server environment.

13. In the next chapter, we will explore **Advanced Security Features** in SQL, covering encryption, user roles, permissions, and securing access to your databases. As data security becomes increasingly important, understanding how to protect your databases from unauthorized access and ensure data privacy will be essential to maintaining a secure system. Let's continue building a secure and optimized database environment! Happy managing your SQL Server tools!

14. Customization and Extensibility are key advantages of using modern SQL Server management tools like **Azure Data Studio** and **SQL Server Management Studio (SSMS)**. Both of these tools allow you to customize your environment to fit your workflow, and extend their functionality with plugins or extensions. In **Azure Data Studio**, for instance, you can add extensions to integrate other data management tools or services, such as Git for version control, or Jupyter Notebooks for running SQL queries alongside code and visualizations.

In **SSMS**, while the environment is more rigid, it does allow for some level of customization. You can adjust settings for things like query execution timeouts, result set formatting, and object explorer filters. Additionally, SSMS allows you to create and run custom scripts, automate tasks, and even extend the tool's functionality using **SQL Server Management Studio Extensions** (SSMSE).

Whether it's adding a new extension to enhance capabilities or adjusting UI settings to better fit your needs, these tools offer the flexibility to accommodate your personal preferences and specific project requirements.

15. Integration with Version Control Systems is another essential feature of modern database management tools. As databases become more complex, managing database schema changes alongside application code becomes critical. **Azure Data Studio** supports **Git integration**, which makes it easy to manage and version control your SQL scripts and database schemas. This integration allows you to store and track changes to your database objects in a Git repository, facilitating collaboration among team members and providing a clear history of changes.

For example, you can work on your database schema changes locally, commit them to a Git repository, and later deploy them to production environments as part of an automated CI/CD pipeline.

16. Query Performance Tuning is a major part of managing SQL Server databases, and the right management tools can help identify slow-running queries and suggest optimizations. **SSMS** provides powerful **query performance analysis** features, including **execution plans** and **query profiler**. These features allow you to visually inspect how SQL Server executes a query, where it spends the most time, and which steps are slowing down your performance.

In SSMS, you can analyze query performance using:

- **Execution Plans**: The query execution plan breaks down the query's execution steps and highlights the most resource-intensive operations (like table scans or sorts), helping you identify opportunities for optimization.

- **SQL Profiler**: SQL Profiler tracks and logs SQL Server events in real-time, providing detailed insights into query performance, query durations, and resources consumed. Using SQL Profiler, you can monitor running queries and adjust them to improve performance.

For example, if you notice that a specific query is causing performance bottlenecks, you can use these tools to identify whether it's performing inefficient operations (like a full table scan) and decide to create an index or rewrite the query to improve performance.

17. Security and Permissions Management are critical aspects of any database system. Proper user management ensures that only authorized users have access to specific data and operations. In **SSMS**, you can manage database security by assigning users to roles and setting **permissions** on database objects like tables, views, and stored procedures. This helps enforce the principle of least privilege — giving users only the access they need to perform their job functions.

Azure Data Studio also offers user management features, although they are more limited than SSMS. However, it can integrate with cloud-based identity management solutions (like Azure Active Directory) to manage user access and enforce role-based access control (RBAC).

In SQL Server, you can manage users with:

- **SQL Server Logins**: These are used to authenticate users to the SQL Server instance.

- **Database Users**: These are mapped to SQL Server logins and grant access to specific databases.

- **Roles**: SQL Server roles help group permissions and simplify user management.

To assign permissions in SSMS:

1. Right-click on the database.

2. Select **Properties**, then go to the **Permissions** tab.

3. Select the user or role and grant or deny specific permissions.

18. Automating Common Tasks is an essential part of database administration. SQL Server offers tools like **SQL Server Agent**, which allows you to automate routine maintenance tasks such as backups, index rebuilding, and query execution. SQL Server Agent can be set up to run jobs at specific times, such as nightly backups or scheduled reports.

In addition to SQL Server Agent, you can use **PowerShell** scripts to automate SQL Server tasks. PowerShell is particularly useful for managing multiple servers or large-scale environments. By writing scripts, you can automate repetitive tasks like creating backups, managing database security, or updating statistics.

Here's a simple example of a PowerShell script to automate a backup:

```powershell
Copy
Backup-SqlDatabase -ServerInstance "your_server" -Database
"your_database" -BackupFile "C:\backups\your_database.bak"
```

This can be scheduled to run at specific intervals, ensuring your backup strategy is followed without manual intervention.

19. Database Deployment and Version Control is another important topic that modern SQL Server tools help with. By using **SSDT** (SQL Server Data Tools) or **Azure Data Studio**, you can streamline the deployment process and integrate your database development into your overall CI/CD pipeline. Both of these tools allow you to **version control** your database schema and deploy changes to production environments in a controlled, repeatable manner.

In **SSDT**, you can use **SQL Server Database Projects** to manage database schema changes, track them in version control systems like Git, and deploy changes to various environments, all while maintaining a history of the changes made. This approach helps ensure that database schema changes are made systematically, with version control providing a clear history of what changes were made and when.

20. Troubleshooting and Diagnostics are essential skills for any database professional, and the management tools discussed in this chapter are instrumental in diagnosing and resolving issues. Whether you're dealing with slow queries, connection problems, or server crashes, **SSMS** and **Azure Data Studio** provide tools for viewing logs, monitoring performance, and identifying the root causes of issues.

In SSMS, for example, you can use the **Activity Monitor** to track real-time performance metrics such as CPU usage, disk activity, and blocking transactions. You can also examine **SQL Server**

logs to identify errors and issues that may need attention. With **SQL Profiler**, you can trace queries that may be causing problems, allowing you to target your optimization efforts more effectively.

21. In conclusion, mastering the **SQL Server Management Tools** and **GUI interfaces** is essential for efficient database management and development. Tools like **SQL Server Management Studio (SSMS)**, **Azure Data Studio**, and **SQL Server Profiler** provide powerful features that help you manage, optimize, and troubleshoot SQL Server instances with ease. By leveraging these tools, you can ensure your SQL Server databases run smoothly, securely, and efficiently.

22. In the next chapter, we will dive into **Advanced Security Features** in SQL, exploring encryption, user roles, and permission management in detail. As your database environment grows, securing your data and ensuring that sensitive information is protected will become even more critical. We'll cover the best practices for database security, including how to configure encryption, manage user access securely, and implement advanced security measures like transparent data encryption (TDE) and column-level encryption.

Understanding SQL Server's security features is essential not just for compliance with data protection regulations, but also for ensuring that your database is resilient against unauthorized access and malicious attacks. We will also look into roles and permissions, so you can control who has access to your database and what actions they can perform. With the increasing need to secure sensitive data, these advanced security practices will help protect your database environment.

In summary, mastering SQL Server's management tools and interfaces, like **SSMS**, **Azure Data Studio**, and **SQLCMD**, allows you to manage your databases effectively, improve query performance, troubleshoot issues, and ensure smooth deployment processes. Whether you're automating tasks with PowerShell, monitoring queries with SQL Profiler, or designing a development pipeline using SSDT, these tools will become an indispensable part of your workflow.

As we transition to the next chapter, let's focus on securing your SQL Server environments to ensure that your data remains not only performant but also protected. Stay tuned for a deep dive into the world of database security, and let's continue building robust, secure, and efficient database systems together! Happy managing and optimizing with your SQL Server tools!

Chapter 24: SQL for Data Warehousing and Business Intelligence

1. Welcome to Chapter 24! In this chapter, we'll explore the world of **Data Warehousing** and **Business Intelligence (BI)**, and how SQL plays a crucial role in these areas. Data Warehousing and BI are essential for organizations that need to consolidate large volumes of data from multiple sources, analyze trends, and make informed business decisions. SQL serves as the backbone for extracting, transforming, and loading (ETL) data into data warehouses, as well as querying that data for insightful analysis. By the end of this chapter, you'll understand how to use SQL for both managing a data warehouse and supporting business intelligence processes.

2. Let's begin with the basics of **Data Warehousing**. A **data warehouse** is a centralized repository that stores large amounts of data from various sources, usually in a format optimized for **analysis** and **reporting**. Unlike operational databases, which are designed to handle transactional workloads (e.g., adding or updating data in real-time), data warehouses are designed for **analytical queries** that aggregate large datasets.

Data warehouses typically use a **dimensional model**, which organizes data into **fact tables** and **dimension tables**. **Fact tables** contain quantitative data (such as sales revenue, profit, or units sold), while **dimension tables** contain descriptive data (such as time, location, or product details). This structure makes it easier to analyze trends, perform aggregations, and create complex reports.

For example, in a sales data warehouse, the **fact table** might include sales figures, and the **dimension tables** would include information about customers, products, and time periods.

3. ETL (Extract, Transform, Load) processes are fundamental to populating data warehouses. The **Extract** step pulls data from multiple source systems (such as transactional databases or flat files). In the **Transform** step, the data is cleaned, enriched, and formatted to fit the structure of the data warehouse. Finally, the **Load** step inserts the transformed data into the warehouse.

SQL plays an important role in all three stages of ETL:

- **Extracting data**: SQL queries are used to retrieve data from operational systems and other sources.

- **Transforming data**: SQL functions, joins, and subqueries help clean, enrich, and format the data for the data warehouse schema.

- **Loading data**: SQL's INSERT INTO and UPDATE statements load the transformed data into the data warehouse.

For example, extracting customer data from an operational database could look like this:

```sql
Copy
SELECT customer_id, customer_name, email, registration_date
FROM customers
WHERE registration_date > '2025-01-01';
```

4. Once the data is loaded into the data warehouse, **Business Intelligence (BI)** tools can be used to analyze the data and generate actionable insights. BI is all about turning raw data into **useful information** that can guide business decisions. BI tools often use SQL queries to generate reports, dashboards, and visualizations, providing decision-makers with a comprehensive view of business performance.

BI typically involves:

- **Data aggregation**: Summarizing large amounts of data (e.g., calculating the total sales revenue by month or by region).

- **Data mining**: Identifying patterns and trends in the data (e.g., detecting customer buying patterns).

- **Reporting**: Generating regular or ad-hoc reports that summarize key metrics.

- **Dashboards**: Visual representations of data, often using charts and graphs.

SQL is used in BI to write queries that aggregate and filter data. For example, calculating total sales by region might look like this:

sql
Copy
```sql
SELECT region, SUM(sales_amount) AS total_sales
FROM sales
GROUP BY region;
```
5. One of the most powerful SQL tools for **Business Intelligence** is the **window function**. Window functions allow you to perform calculations across a set of rows related to the current row, without collapsing the data into a single row (as GROUP BY does). This is extremely useful for calculating running totals, moving averages, and ranking data.

For example, to calculate a running total of sales by month, you can use the SUM() window function:

sql
Copy
```sql
SELECT month, sales_amount,
       SUM(sales_amount) OVER (ORDER BY month) AS
running_total
FROM sales
ORDER BY month;
```
In this query, the SUM() function is applied to all previous rows in the result set, generating a running total of sales by month. Window functions make it easy to analyze trends over time without losing the detailed row-level information.

6. ETL Performance Optimization is critical when working with large datasets in data warehousing and business intelligence projects. SQL plays an essential role in making ETL processes efficient. To optimize ETL performance, it's important to keep the following best practices in mind:

- **Batch Processing**: Instead of processing all the data in one large operation, break it down into smaller batches. This prevents database locking issues and improves the overall processing speed. For example, instead of inserting all rows from a staging table into a data warehouse at once, you can insert them in smaller batches of, say, 1000 rows at a time.

- **Indexing**: Ensure that the tables involved in ETL processes, especially the fact tables, are properly indexed. Indexing can significantly speed up the extraction and transformation processes, making it easier to pull data from source systems and load it into the data warehouse.

- **Parallel Processing**: Many databases support parallel processing, which can be a great way to speed up the ETL process when dealing with large amounts of data. By running multiple extraction or transformation tasks in parallel, you can take full advantage of the available system resources.

- **Incremental Loading**: Rather than reloading the entire dataset every time, use incremental loading techniques. Only load new or changed records to reduce the time and resources needed for each ETL cycle.

For example, rather than doing a full load, you can use a `WHERE` clause to only extract records that have been updated since the last ETL cycle:

sql
Copy
```sql
SELECT * FROM source_table
WHERE last_modified > '2025-04-01';
```
This helps keep your ETL process more efficient by only processing new or changed data.

7. Data Aggregation is another key concept in data warehousing and business intelligence. SQL's ability to aggregate data efficiently is vital for producing meaningful reports and insights. The **GROUP BY** clause is used to summarize data across different dimensions, such as calculating total sales per region, average order value by customer, or total revenue by product category.

In a typical data warehouse, you may need to aggregate facts like sales, revenue, or inventory quantities across different time periods or geographic regions. SQL's `SUM()`, `AVG()`, `MAX()`, `MIN()`, and other aggregate functions are designed specifically for these tasks. For example, to calculate total sales by region:

sql
Copy
```sql
SELECT region, SUM(sales_amount) AS total_sales
FROM sales_fact
GROUP BY region;
```
Aggregating data can be combined with **filters** (using the `WHERE` clause) or **window functions** to perform advanced analytics, such as running totals or moving averages.

8. Business Intelligence Reporting typically involves more complex queries and aggregations to help decision-makers understand business performance. SQL plays an essential role in this process by generating detailed reports and dashboards, which are often the foundation for **BI tools** like **Power BI**, **Tableau**, or **Looker**.

To generate useful reports, SQL is used to create complex queries that:

- Aggregate data across multiple dimensions (e.g., calculating total sales by product, time, or region).

- Join data from multiple tables, including fact and dimension tables.

- Use **subqueries** or **CTEs (Common Table Expressions)** to organize complex logic and improve query readability.

For instance, a more complex query might look like this:

sql
Copy
```
WITH SalesSummary AS (
    SELECT region, product_id, SUM(sales_amount) AS
total_sales
    FROM sales_fact
    GROUP BY region, product_id
)
SELECT s.region, p.product_name, ss.total_sales
FROM SalesSummary ss
JOIN products p ON ss.product_id = p.product_id
WHERE ss.total_sales > 100000
ORDER BY ss.total_sales DESC;
```
In this query, a **CTE** (`SalesSummary`) is used to aggregate sales by region and product. The main query then joins this summary with the `products` dimension table to get the product name, and filters the results to show only products with sales greater than $100,000.

9. Data Visualization is an essential part of Business Intelligence. While SQL alone cannot provide interactive charts or graphs, it plays an integral role in **preparing the data** for visualization in BI tools. Once SQL queries aggregate and summarize data, the results can be imported into BI tools, which can then create interactive dashboards, pie charts, bar graphs, and other visual elements that help users interpret and make decisions based on the data.

For example, you might query the data warehouse to get sales totals by region and then use a BI tool to visualize that data in a geographical heat map, showing how sales are distributed across different regions.

10. OLAP Cubes and Multidimensional Queries: In more complex BI environments, OLAP (Online Analytical Processing) cubes provide fast query performance by pre-aggregating data. While OLAP is traditionally a separate tool, SQL plays a significant role in querying multidimensional data and generating reports from OLAP systems.

In SQL-based BI solutions, you may create cube-like structures using `GROUP BY` and `HAVING` to aggregate data across multiple dimensions. However, true OLAP cubes are typically built using specialized software (like **SQL Server Analysis Services** or **Oracle OLAP**), which can be queried using **MDX (Multidimensional Expressions)** or **SQL**.

Here's an example of how you might query an OLAP-like structure with SQL:

sql
Copy
```sql
SELECT product_category, YEAR(sales_date) AS sales_year,
SUM(sales_amount) AS total_sales
FROM sales_fact
GROUP BY product_category, YEAR(sales_date)
ORDER BY product_category, sales_year;
```
This query aggregates sales data by product category and year, which is similar to how an OLAP cube might structure data for multidimensional analysis.

11. Data Mining is another crucial aspect of Business Intelligence. SQL is used to pull raw data from a data warehouse, which can then be fed into **data mining** algorithms that identify patterns, trends, and anomalies. While SQL is not typically the tool for building machine learning models or data mining algorithms, it is used to prepare data for analysis.

For example, you might use SQL to query sales data over time and then apply machine learning algorithms outside of SQL (in Python, R, or specialized BI tools) to predict future sales trends, customer behavior, or market conditions. However, basic **trend analysis** and **forecasting** can often be done directly in SQL by using window functions or time series analysis.

12. Data Quality remains a vital concern in data warehousing and BI. If the data in your warehouse is inaccurate or incomplete, your analysis and reports will be flawed. SQL plays a significant role in ensuring that data quality is maintained throughout the ETL process. Data validation rules, error checking, and cleaning operations can all be implemented using SQL.

You can use SQL to identify data quality issues, such as duplicate records, missing values, or inconsistent formatting. For instance, to find duplicate records:

sql
Copy
```sql
SELECT customer_id, COUNT(*)
FROM customers
GROUP BY customer_id
```

```
HAVING COUNT(*) > 1;
```
This query identifies customers with duplicate records, allowing you to clean the data before loading it into the warehouse.

13. In conclusion, **SQL for Data Warehousing and Business Intelligence** is indispensable for managing and analyzing large datasets. Whether you're using SQL to build and populate a data warehouse, aggregate data for reporting, or prepare data for advanced analysis, SQL remains a powerful and essential tool in every step of the process. Mastering these techniques allows you to support data-driven decision-making and help organizations leverage their data for competitive advantage.

14. In the next chapter, we will explore **Advanced Security Features** in SQL, focusing on encryption, roles, permissions, and secure access management. As your databases store more sensitive data, security becomes a key concern. We will delve into best practices for securing your SQL Server environments and ensuring that sensitive data is protected. Let's continue building secure and optimized systems! Happy warehousing and analyzing!

14. As we've seen throughout this chapter, SQL is not just a tool for basic querying; it's an essential component of a successful **data warehousing** and **business intelligence** strategy. With SQL, you can design efficient ETL processes, perform data transformations, aggregate and analyze large datasets, and ensure high-quality data for reporting and decision-making. From **basic aggregations** to **advanced analytical functions** like window functions and OLAP querying, SQL plays a central role in turning raw data into actionable insights.

By mastering these techniques, you can help organizations make data-driven decisions, detect trends and patterns, and optimize business processes. Whether you are managing data in a large-scale **data warehouse**, building reports and dashboards for business users, or preparing data for machine learning models, SQL is the foundation of most modern data operations.

15. In the next chapter, we will dive into **Advanced Security Features** in SQL. As your data warehouse and BI systems grow, securing your sensitive data becomes even more critical. We'll explore encryption methods, how to manage user roles and permissions, and best practices for database security. Securing your SQL environment is essential not just for protecting sensitive business information, but also for complying with data privacy regulations and maintaining the integrity of your system.

Let's continue building secure and scalable data systems while ensuring the privacy and security of the valuable data at the heart of your business. Ready to enhance your skills in **SQL security**? Let's get started! Happy querying, aggregating, and analyzing!

Chapter 25: Best Practices, Debugging, and Future SQL Trends

1. Welcome to Chapter 25! In this chapter, we'll explore some essential **best practices** for writing efficient, maintainable, and secure SQL queries. Additionally, we'll look at **debugging techniques** to help you troubleshoot SQL issues and improve performance. Finally, we'll discuss some of the **future trends in SQL** that will shape the way we work with databases in the coming years. By the end of this chapter, you'll have the knowledge to not only write high-quality SQL but also stay ahead of emerging trends in the world of database management.

2. Let's begin with **Best Practices**. Adhering to best practices when writing SQL queries helps ensure that your code is **efficient**, **maintainable**, and **secure**. Whether you're working with small or large datasets, these best practices will help you avoid common pitfalls and optimize performance.

Use Descriptive Naming Conventions: Naming conventions are crucial for making your queries and database schema easier to understand and maintain. For instance, use clear names for tables and columns that reflect the data they store. Avoid using ambiguous names like `data`, `temp`, or `info`, and instead use names like `sales`, `customers`, and `product_categories`.

For example, instead of using:

```sql
Copy
SELECT * FROM data;
```
Use:

```sql
Copy
SELECT * FROM sales_transactions;
```
This makes your SQL more readable and understandable for other team members or developers who may work with the database in the future.

3. **Limit the Use of SELECT ***: While it's tempting to use `SELECT *` to retrieve all columns from a table, this practice can lead to performance issues, especially when working with large tables. Retrieving unnecessary columns can slow down your queries, especially when working with databases containing millions or even billions of rows. Instead, always select only the columns you need:

```sql
Copy
SELECT customer_id, customer_name, total_purchase FROM
customers WHERE country = 'USA';
```
This reduces the amount of data transferred and speeds up query execution.

4. Indexing for Performance: Proper indexing is key to improving the performance of your queries, especially when working with large datasets. Indexes allow SQL to quickly locate data, reducing the need for full table scans. Be strategic about indexing: index columns used in `WHERE` clauses, `JOIN` conditions, and `ORDER BY` clauses.

However, be cautious not to over-index your tables, as excessive indexes can slow down `INSERT`, `UPDATE`, and `DELETE` operations. Always test and monitor your queries to ensure that indexing is improving performance rather than causing unnecessary overhead.

5. Use Joins Efficiently: Joins are a powerful feature of SQL, but they can lead to poor performance if not used properly. Here are a few tips:

- **Prefer INNER JOINs over OUTER JOINs** when you don't need unmatched rows from either table.

- When joining large tables, ensure that join conditions are indexed to speed up lookups.

- Avoid joining tables unnecessarily; use subqueries or **Common Table Expressions (CTEs)** when needed for clarity and performance.

For example, an inefficient query that joins unnecessary tables might look like this:

sql
Copy
```sql
SELECT * FROM orders
INNER JOIN customers ON orders.customer_id =
customers.customer_id
INNER JOIN employees ON orders.employee_id =
employees.employee_id;
```
If you only need the order details, you can eliminate the unnecessary join to the `employees` table, improving performance:

sql
Copy
```sql
SELECT order_id, customer_id, order_date FROM orders;
```
6. SQL Injection Protection: One of the most important aspects of SQL best practices is ensuring your queries are secure. **SQL injection** is one of the most common security vulnerabilities, where malicious users can input harmful SQL code into your queries, compromising your database. Always use **parameterized queries** or **prepared statements** to protect your database from SQL injection attacks.

For example, using a parameterized query in **SQL Server**:

sql
Copy
```sql
DECLARE @customer_id INT = 123;
SELECT customer_name, email FROM customers WHERE
customer_id = @customer_id;
```
This method prevents attackers from injecting malicious SQL code into the query.

7. Use Transactions for Data Integrity: SQL transactions ensure that a series of queries either **complete successfully** or **fail together**, maintaining the integrity of your data. Always use transactions when you need to perform multiple actions that must all succeed or fail together, such as transferring money from one account to another.

Here's an example of a basic transaction:

```sql
Copy
BEGIN TRANSACTION;

UPDATE accounts SET balance = balance - 100 WHERE
account_id = 1;
UPDATE accounts SET balance = balance + 100 WHERE
account_id = 2;

-- If no errors, commit the transaction
COMMIT;

-- If there's an error, rollback the transaction
ROLLBACK;
```
This ensures that the database remains in a consistent state, even in the event of an error.

8. Debugging SQL Queries: Debugging SQL queries is essential for identifying and resolving issues with query logic, performance, or data integrity. Here are some debugging techniques to help:

- Use **EXPLAIN or EXPLAIN PLAN** to analyze how SQL Server executes your queries. This helps identify slow-performing parts of a query, such as full table scans or inefficient joins.

- **Check for Data Type Mismatches**: SQL errors often occur when there are mismatched data types between columns and values being inserted or updated. Use explicit type casting if necessary to ensure data consistency.

- **Isolate Problematic Queries**: If a query runs slowly or returns incorrect results, isolate it and test it with smaller data sets. This helps you narrow down the issue and find the root cause more easily.

- **Use Profiler or Query Analyzer**: Tools like **SQL Server Profiler** and **Query Analyzer** allow you to trace and monitor queries, giving you a deeper insight into performance problems or unexpected behavior.

9. Avoid Nested Loops and Complex Subqueries: In complex queries, especially those involving multiple joins or subqueries, it's easy to end up with nested loops or overly complicated queries that can be difficult to debug and optimize. Instead, try breaking down your queries into smaller, manageable parts. Use **CTEs** or temporary tables to simplify complex logic.

For example, rather than writing a deeply nested subquery:

```sql
Copy
SELECT order_id FROM orders WHERE customer_id = (SELECT
customer_id FROM customers WHERE last_name = 'Smith');
```
You can rewrite it using a **CTE**:

```sql
Copy
WITH Customer AS (
    SELECT customer_id FROM customers WHERE last_name =
'Smith'
)
SELECT order_id FROM orders WHERE customer_id IN (SELECT
customer_id FROM Customer);
```
This improves readability and performance.

10. Future SQL Trends: SQL continues to evolve, and several key trends are shaping the future of database management:

- **Cloud Databases**: With the growing adoption of cloud computing, more organizations are migrating their databases to the cloud. Cloud platforms like **Amazon RDS**, **Azure SQL Database**, and **Google Cloud SQL** offer managed database services that handle scalability, performance optimization, and backup management. SQL remains a key tool for querying and managing these cloud-based systems.

- **NoSQL and SQL Integration**: While NoSQL databases (like MongoDB or Cassandra) are growing in popularity for handling unstructured data, SQL is still widely used for relational data. The future trend is the integration of **SQL and NoSQL** systems, allowing organizations to leverage the strengths of both. Technologies like **SQL-on-Hadoop** and **SQL-on-NoSQL** are bridging the gap between relational and non-relational data models.

- **Machine Learning Integration**: SQL Server and other database systems are increasingly integrating with machine learning platforms. This allows data scientists and developers to build machine learning models directly within the database using **T-SQL** or **Python/R** scripts embedded within SQL queries.

- **Automation**: With advancements in automation, SQL databases are becoming smarter in terms of self-healing, scaling, and optimizing queries without human intervention. Automation tools like **SQL Server Management Studio** and **Azure Data Studio** are evolving to incorporate more intelligent performance tuning and database management features.

- **Graph Databases**: SQL databases are also expanding into graph data models, which are useful for applications like social networks, recommendation systems, and fraud detection. **SQL Server 2017** and beyond provide support for graph data types and queries, expanding SQL's utility in non-relational contexts.

11. In conclusion, following **best practices** and learning how to debug and optimize SQL queries will help you become more effective at managing databases, solving problems, and maintaining performance. As SQL continues to evolve, staying on top of the latest trends—such as cloud databases, machine learning, and NoSQL integration—will allow you to keep your skills sharp and your database systems modern and efficient.

12. In the next chapter, we will explore **SQL for Data Security**, focusing on how to secure your databases, manage access control, and protect sensitive data using encryption and other methods. With data security becoming increasingly important in today's digital landscape, understanding how to secure your SQL environment will be essential to protecting your organization's information. Let's continue building secure and optimized database systems together! Happy querying, debugging, and preparing for the future of SQL!

13. Performance Tuning will always be a crucial skill for any SQL professional. As database sizes grow and data volumes increase, writing efficient queries and optimizing performance becomes more important. Performance tuning encompasses various strategies, including query optimization, index management, and server resource management. To keep performance at its peak, consider the following:

- **Query Optimization**: Focus on writing efficient SQL queries by avoiding unnecessary subqueries, minimizing the use of `SELECT *`, and leveraging joins effectively.

- **Indexing**: Proper indexing can make a huge difference in query performance, but over-indexing can also be detrimental. Monitor index usage regularly to remove unused or redundant indexes.

- **Database Design**: Normalize your data where necessary, but also balance it with denormalization for read-heavy workloads where performance is critical. Choose between **star schema** and **snowflake schema** based on your data warehouse needs.

- **Resource Allocation**: Ensure that your server has sufficient memory, CPU, and disk resources, and that your database is tuned for optimal I/O performance. Monitoring tools can alert you to resource bottlenecks and help you allocate resources more effectively.

Tools like **SQL Profiler**, **Execution Plans**, and **Query Performance Tuning** are invaluable in pinpointing the exact performance bottlenecks, whether it's a poor index design or inefficient query structure.

14. Debugging Techniques are an essential part of the development and maintenance cycle. Being able to identify and fix issues quickly is a critical skill for database professionals. SQL debugging typically involves tracing query execution, analyzing error messages, and understanding why certain queries are not behaving as expected.

Here are some common debugging techniques:

- **Break Down Complex Queries**: If a query is returning unexpected results, break it down into smaller parts and test each component. Start by isolating the issue (e.g., a particular join or aggregation) and progressively add more complexity to narrow down the cause of the issue.

- **Error Handling**: Use **TRY...CATCH** blocks in SQL Server to catch errors and handle them gracefully. This can help identify specific error conditions and allow you to control how errors are managed within your code.

sql
Copy
```
BEGIN TRY
    -- Code that may cause an error
    SELECT * FROM non_existing_table;
END TRY
BEGIN CATCH
    -- Handle the error
    PRINT 'An error occurred: ' + ERROR_MESSAGE();
END CATCH;
```
- **Use Logging**: Create logging mechanisms to capture the execution flow of your SQL queries. This can be particularly useful in complex stored procedures or triggers.

15. SQL Server Query Store is a powerful tool for tracking query performance over time. It stores historical data about query execution plans and allows you to track changes in performance. By enabling the **Query Store**, you can identify slow-performing queries, analyze execution plan changes, and even force specific query plans to improve performance.

Enabling the Query Store can help you track regressions and prevent performance issues from escalating. It provides data on both the logical and physical operations of queries, making it easier to pinpoint the cause of slowdowns.

16. Emerging SQL Trends are shaping the future of database management. As technology evolves, new approaches to managing and interacting with SQL databases are emerging. Here are a few trends that will define the future of SQL:

- **Cloud Databases**: Cloud-based solutions such as **Amazon RDS**, **Azure SQL Database**, and **Google Cloud SQL** offer scalable, flexible environments that reduce the need for on-premise hardware and simplify database management. With cloud databases, you can easily scale your storage, optimize performance, and reduce administrative overhead.

- **Serverless Computing**: The **serverless model** allows databases to automatically scale up or down based on demand without requiring manual intervention. SQL databases are increasingly moving towards this model, enabling cost-effective and scalable solutions.

- **Multi-Model Databases**: Multi-model databases that combine relational, graph, document, and key-value data models are gaining traction. SQL will increasingly integrate with NoSQL models, allowing users to choose the right approach for different types of data within a single platform.

- **AI and Machine Learning Integration**: SQL databases are becoming more integrated with **AI** and **machine learning** platforms. For instance, **SQL Server Machine Learning Services** lets you run R or Python scripts directly within SQL queries. This trend is opening new doors for more advanced analytics, predictive modeling, and real-time decision-making.

- **Automation and Self-Optimizing Databases**: SQL Server and other database management systems are becoming more automated, with self-tuning features that optimize performance based on workload patterns. This trend aims to reduce the manual effort required for database maintenance, making it easier to manage large-scale systems.

17. Data Privacy and Compliance will continue to play a major role in SQL development. As data privacy regulations like **GDPR** and **CCPA** become stricter, understanding how to secure sensitive data using SQL will be increasingly important. The ability to **encrypt** data, **anonymize** it, and manage **access control** through roles and permissions will be crucial for database professionals.

Many SQL platforms now support **data encryption** at rest and in transit, as well as more granular **role-based access control** (RBAC) for managing who can access sensitive data. SQL queries will need to incorporate these security measures to ensure compliance and protect customer data.

18. NoSQL and SQL Convergence: As the need for handling unstructured data grows, the lines between SQL and NoSQL databases are starting to blur. Some SQL databases now provide built-in support for semi-structured data formats like **JSON** and **XML**, allowing for flexibility in storing and querying data that doesn't fit neatly into a relational structure.

For instance, **PostgreSQL** and **MySQL** support **JSON** data types, and **SQL Server** has improved its handling of **JSON** and **XML** data with functions like `JSON_VALUE` and `OPENJSON`. This convergence is making it easier to manage diverse data models using a unified SQL approach.

19. SQL and Big Data: The rise of **big data** analytics is another trend that will affect SQL. Many SQL platforms are adapting to handle large-scale data processing workloads. Platforms like **Apache Hive** and **Google BigQuery** use SQL-like query languages to interact with massive datasets, enabling SQL-based querying on big data.

SQL Server and other databases are increasingly supporting **parallel processing**, **distributed query execution**, and **in-memory databases** to handle large-scale data analytics. As SQL becomes more integrated into big data ecosystems, its ability to process and analyze large volumes of data will continue to evolve.

20. In conclusion, **Best Practices**, **Debugging**, and **Future Trends** are all essential areas of focus for any SQL professional. Writing efficient, secure, and maintainable SQL queries ensures that your database systems are both optimized and safe. Debugging skills will help you troubleshoot issues quickly, while staying updated on emerging trends like cloud computing, AI, and NoSQL integration will keep your skills relevant and help you manage the next generation of database systems.

As we move forward, **SQL** will continue to evolve, incorporating more advanced features and capabilities. Whether you're working with traditional relational databases, big data platforms, or hybrid systems, understanding best practices and keeping up with trends will ensure that you are prepared for the future of database management.

21. In the next chapter, we will dive deeper into **SQL for Data Security**, focusing on securing your databases, managing user access, and protecting sensitive information with encryption and other methods. As the amount of sensitive data in your systems grows, securing that data becomes increasingly important. We'll explore best practices and techniques for ensuring your SQL environment is safe, compliant, and well-secured. Let's continue building secure, scalable, and efficient database systems together! Happy optimizing, debugging, and preparing for the future of SQL!